PARTNERSHIP

WOMEN & MEN IN MINISTRY

Fran
FERDER
&
John
HEAGLE

AVE MARIA PRESS Notre Dame, IN 46556

Fran Ferder, a member of the Franciscan Sisters of Perpetual Adoration, and **Rev. John Heagle** are co-directors of the Therapy and Renewal Associates, a ministerial counseling and consultation service for the Archdiocese of Seattle. They both teach at the Institute for Theological Studies at Seattle University in the SUMORE program and maintain active national speaking schedules.

Ferder holds a master's and a Ph.D. in Clinical Psychology from Loyola University of Chicago, and a Doctorate in Ministry from the Aquinas Institute of Theology. She is the author of *Words Made Flesh* (Ave Maria Press) and *Called to Break Bread* (Quixote Center Publications).

Heagle, ordained for the Diocese of LaCrosse, WI, has had more than two decades of pastoral experience. For the last 15 years he has also been engaged in retreat and renewal ministry. He is the author of five books on Christian spirituality, including *Life to the Full, On the Way* and *Suffering and Evil* (Thomas More Press).

© 1989 by Ave Maria Press, Notre Dame, IN 46556

International Standard Book Number: 0-87793-399-5

Library of Congress Catalog Card Number: 88-83596

Printed and Bound in the United States of America.

To our parents

Audrey and Jacob J. Ferder
Alice and John J. Heagle

**in loving gratitude for the partnership
they have modeled in their lives**

Contents

Introduction

Write Down the Vision

In his novel *Hawaii* James Michener tells a story
about the important relationship between male and female gods to the people of the island.

The people of Bora Bora set out on a voyage to the island to the north. On arrival, they realized they had left
their female god behind. Going back to retrieve her
seemed out of the question, so the people resolved to face
the future without her.

However, after repeated attempts to live peacefully
and successfully on the new island failed, they decided to
return to Bora Bora and bring back the female god. Their
preparation for the voyage had been incomplete. They
had forgotten some vital presence. "We have left behind
the goddess Pere," they concluded, "the goddess of the
flame who directs our lives, the most ancient of goddesses." It was Teroro who decided to return for her. "I
am going to bring back the stone of Pere," Teroro explained. "I think the island should have not only men
gods, but women gods too."

Not only men gods. Could it be that these ancient
people understood something about the divine that we
have yet to grasp? Could it be that the women and men
we so easily dismiss as "pagan" had powerful insights

about the sacred that we have missed? Obviously, we are not polytheists with a basketful of gods and goddesses at our disposal. But we are women and men made in the image of a God who mirrored something of both maleness and femaleness in creating us. Perhaps, like the early inhabitants of Michener's *Hawaii*, something about our voyage has been incomplete. Perhaps our attempts to live peacefully and successfully have failed because some vital presence is missing. Perhaps our earth "should have not only men gods, but women gods too."

If the ancient people of Bora Bora touched an elemental truth as they reflected on their experience, our own times call us to a similar process of reflection and a re-winning of that vital truth if we are to survive.

Scanning the horizon of our church and our world, what do we see? What realities compel our attention? What symbols dominate our religious and cultural lives?

—— a male God we call father

—— a hierarchical decision-making body in Catholicism, which is presided over by a male priesthood

—— a "natural resemblance to Christ" based on being male rather than being human and Christian

—— a morality defined primarily by males, based on moral absolutes and emphasizing the "objective" rightness or wrongness of particular actions, regardless of the situation

—— a language system founded on male imagery and metaphors

—— a strong patriarchal bias in church law and practice

—— a system of international law and diplomacy that reflects a predominantly male approach to political and social realities

—— an ever increasing accumulation of destructive weapons that places human survival at risk

—— a weary earth that staggers under the unbal-

anced weight of glass skyscrapers in one direction and cardboard hovels in the other

—— an even wearier people ravaged by one nation's
conquests and oppressed by another's achieve-
ments

Some contemporary social commentators and theologians suggest that the root of these problems lies in the
loss of the "feminine symbol"—the absence of a model of
nurturance, inclusion, gentleness and transformation,
in contrast to the domination of the masculine model of
aggression, conquest and violence.

Other thinkers find the terms "masculine" and
"feminine" too limiting. They believe the problems that
confront our world and our church cannot adequately be
described as an imbalance of power between gender stereotypes, but are related instead to a style of moral reasoning and decision-making that overemphasizes competition and de-emphasizes relational qualities. They
prefer to talk about the need to regain the *human* rather
than the "feminine"—to recapture the values of compassion, cooperation and mutuality. These values reveal the
depth of what it means to be human; they are not gender
specific.

The attempts to understand our present crisis may
vary, but beneath the differing interpretations is an emerging conviction, a truth we can no longer deny. Something is missing. An essential quality of wisdom and
compassion is lacking. Our times call us to return to our
history and collective human experience in order to recover something essential, something to do with a "relational presence," a sense of our primordial bonds with
one another and with the earth, a willingness to share responsibility for life.

But this should not be just a journey into the past. It
should be a voyage of creativity, a commitment to shape
our future together. It involves the search for a new vision regarding human relationships, a collaborative
journey toward global community.

This book is written in the hope of contributing to

this journey of recovery and exploration. It is an attempt to read our sacred stories with new eyes and fresh insight. It seeks to recover in our faith tradition the ancient vision of partnership between women and men in order to enflesh it in the emerging church. It also reaches out to the future. The pages that follow are an invitation to reimagine the church as a community of disciples who journey in hope and who minister in mutuality.

On the level of theological reflection and official church teaching, the interest in ministerial partnership between women and men is at best tentative. In a rather courageous step, the bishops of the United States are bringing the topic into public dialogue through their letter *"Partners in the Mystery of Redemption: A Pastoral Response to Women's Concerns for Church and Society,"* which, as this book is being written, is in its first draft. Pope John Paul II has also written a pastoral letter on women. Despite these developments, a universal commitment to partnership ministry remains a distant dream, a vision waiting to be recognized and affirmed.

This is not the case, however, on the pastoral level. The burgeoning of ministries since Vatican II, combined with the growing shortage of priests, has provided a spontaneous laboratory for collaborative ministry. More than that, it has created a grassroots movement for ministerial partnership. Unfortunately, the wider institutional church often responds to this movement with suspicion and fear.

How can this fear of mutuality be translated into openness? How can the distant dream of partnership become a reality? How do we enflesh the vision?

The most important answer to these questions lies with the grassroots movement itself. Genuine mutuality between women and men in the church will come about because people with courage and commitment continue to believe in it and to live it in local communities of faith. In addition to the lived experience is the ongoing task of reading the signs of the times, of listening to the needs of God's people, and of discerning the direction of the Spirit.

Beyond these efforts is still another way of giving birth to the dream and of enfleshing the vision. We speak here of the responsibility to tell the story as it unfolds, the challenge of naming our experience in the flow of history. When the seventh-century prophet Habakkuk became discouraged with what seemed to be the limited influence of God's word, Yahweh gave him this advice:

> "Write down the vision
> clearly upon the tablets,
>   so that one can read it readily.
> For the vision still has its time,
>   presses on to fulfillment, and will
>   not disappoint"
>   (Hb 2:2, *NAB*).

This book is a way of responding to this same challenge in our time. Like Habakkuk, we feel compelled to "write down the vision." We want to help recover what we have lost. We seek to share in the task of articulating the dream of the future church.

Given the condition of our world and our church, this is not a casual commitment. An urgency surrounds all of our lives today, an urgency that calls for discernment and decisive action.

Today, more than ever before, as weapons of destruction are stockpiled deep in the earth's green farmland and emerald oceans, we need a symbol of gentleness to call us back from our overbalanced reliance on aggression.

As thousands of helpless people are tortured by terrorists, and rendered helpless by opportunists, we need a symbol of warmth to call us back from our indifference.

As women continue to be excluded from sacramental ministry and decision making in the church; as theologians who hear a different voice are investigated and reprimanded; as some segments of church leadership continue to emphasize discipline over compassion, and to place more importance on the observance of laws than on the lived experience of the people, our church needs a symbol of nurturance to call us back from legalism.

Our world and our church need women and men in leadership who listen, feel, need and care; women and men who want to share journeys more than they want to enforce rules; women and men who are not afraid to admit that perhaps "only men gods" are not sufficient to bring peace to island earth. We need women and men who are vulnerable enough to know that maleness does not completely image the divine and courageous enough to go back to recover that vital presence we name female.

A recovery of female presence in world and church decision making does not imply a negation of man's role. What is needed is a new kind of male-female partnership, not a new form of male-female rivalry.

Precisely what is such a partnership and what does it look like? This book is based on the conviction that God created human beings in God's image as male and female to share responsibility for tending the earth and its creatures. Partnership, then, is that holy and primordial stance of full equality and mutuality that women and men must have before each other, before the earth and before the God in whose likeness they are created.

In describing partnership further, it might be helpful to clarify what it is not. Partnership is not a romantic pairing of ministers. It is not "coupling for the kingdom" as some cynics have wryly suggested. Nor is it a convenient biblical excuse for infatuated twosomes looking for a ministerial rationale for their togetherness. The expression of partnership is not confined to male-female combinations, nor can it be presumed in situations where an equal number of men minister alongside of an equal number of women.

Partnership is not so much a manifestation of equality in numbers, as it is an expression of equality in attitude. Consider the following: Mary and Bill work together in a parish. They pride themselves in having a "partnership" ministry and talk about the importance of being a "team." Yet in actual practice Bill makes all of the decisions, freely gives Mary directives and orders (which she dutifully obeys) and occupies a position of prominence in all parish functions. When people have a question, they know they must address Bill. Mary works hard as a background planner, organizer and fill-in person. She is deferent toward Bill and the two of them operate much like a boss and his lackey. Even though we have a male and a female person engaged in ministry and seeming to get along well together, we do not have a team and we do not have an authentic expression of biblical partnership.

Consider a second situation: Sue and Jim are co-directors of a retreat center. They hold regular staff meetings in which all planning and decision making is shared. Each person's opinion is respected by the other and each has an equal chance of influencing the outcome of decisions. Conflicts and differences are discussed openly; both "nitty-gritty" and more important tasks are evenly shared. An inner attitude of mutuality, as opposed to self-sufficiency, characterizes their interactions. Other women and men on the staff are consulted, respected and valued.

Genuine biblical partnership involves people in shared interaction, people who do not treat each other differently because of sexual differences. Partnership is the antithesis of sexism. It values, respects and is receptive to all women and men, not because they are females or males, but because they are equally human and equally expressive of God's image.

At the same time, a kind of creative tension exists in biblical partnership. On the one hand, it is a mystery that transcends gender and finds its authentic expression in mature, committed disciples, regardless of their sex. On the other hand, because God's people are made up of two distinct sexes, genuine biblical partnership must continually seek to manifest this complementary relationship in concrete forms, particularly at levels of leadership and decision making.

The personal and collective commitment to collaboration is vital to our continued existence. It is impossible to approach people of other nations as partners, or the earth as a partner, when we have lost that sense of connectedness with each other—a loss most painfully visible in the very Christian tradition that ought to sustain us in partnership.

1
Shaking the Foundations
The Emergence of the Partnership Movement

In the fall of 1987 the Prescott Memorial Baptist Church in Memphis, Tennessee, called Nancy Hastings Sehested to be their senior pastor. The daughter and granddaughter of Southern Baptist ministers, Nancy had always had a sense that God was calling her into the service of the gospel. She was not necessarily anticipating, however, that her vocation would become an occasion of controversy in the church.

When the local Southern Baptist Association challenged her right to be a pastor and asked her by what authority she was preaching the word of God, Nancy's response was simple and direct. She recalled the tradition of faith and ministry in her family. She shared her convictions regarding the gospel as a call to discipleship and service. Finally, she spoke of the example of Jesus at the last supper as he took the towel and the basin of water to model the meaning of true servanthood. By what right did Nancy respond to the call to be a pastor? By what authority does she preach the gospel? Because, as Nancy put it, "I found a towel with my name on it."

Nancy Hastings Sehested is a striking example of an

emerging movement in our society and in the church. She is symbolic of the millions of women who have "found a towel with their name on it," and who are claiming their role in helping to shape the future of the human story. This movement is not limited to ministry or the issue of women's leadership in communities of faith. It is reflected in the women who are seeking greater participation in education, medicine, law, politics, business and the other areas of cultural endeavor.

Even more importantly, this movement is not limited to women. It breaks through the usual barriers of gender, race, religious background and social class to embrace all people who want to collaborate in building a community of compassion on this planet. It transcends the polarization and fear that so frequently prevent women and men from working together and supporting each other. This shift toward partnership reaffirms marriage as a covenantal bond; it places a new value on shared parenting and the ministry of family; it calls for a new mutuality between women and men who collaborate in parish ministry. In short, this movement proclaims that each of us has a towel with our name on it.

In this chapter we want to explore the meaning of this contemporary movement toward partnership between women and men. First, we will examine the significance of the movement in its relationship to other global and ecclesial issues; next, we will trace the recent development of the partnership vision, especially as it is growing within the contemporary Catholic community; finally, we will address some of the preliminary implications of this grassroots quest for collaboration.

The Significance of the Partnership Movement

In the last several decades we have become aware of an intensity about our age that evades our comprehension and challenges our imagination. Instinctively we recognize that the human community is moving through a turning point in its history. The solutions of the past are no longer adequate for the demands of the present. The questions are more perplexing, the stakes higher, the obstacles more formidable.

The mystics and artists tell us that we are experiencing a transformation of our language and symbols, a leap of human consciousness. Political commentators speak of a shift in the global configuration of power and the need to develop structures for the emerging international community. Popular psychology invites us to find better ways to manage stress and to develop a more holistic approach to life. Theologians and cultural philosophers grope for words to describe what is taking place. We hear of "future shock" and "psychic numbing"; we are told of "axial periods" and "paradigm shifts."

Our words seem inadequate. Our language falters. But the flow of information continues, like a swelling river of data and decisions that at times threatens to overwhelm us. In the face of cataclysmic change we are challenged to develop a new world-view and a new basis for self-understanding. Writing more than a quarter of a century ago, Kenneth Boulding, the prominent economist and environmentalist, observed that "if the human race is to survive, it will have to change its ways of thinking more in the next 25 years than in the last 25,000."

It appears that we still have a long way to go in this journey of transformation. Even as we move toward a new millennium, the pain and the promise of this century is still poignantly with us. We carry its anguish and its hopes and its unfinished dreams. We are haunted by its memories and possibilities: the wrenching tragedy of two world wars; the lingering scars of Vietnam on our national psyche; the space program and the technological explosion; the transformation of our global communications system; the grassroots movements to overcome political oppression among the poor and dispossessed; international terror and violence. All of these reflect a time of transition and upheaval that may be unparalleled in recent history.

As we look to the future, the human community is confronted with issues that are crucial to its future growth and survival. At the present rate the world population is doubling approximately every 20 years; our natural resources are dwindling; every day thousands die from malnourishment, disease or violence. We live under the threat of nuclear destruction and the widespread pollution of our environment. There is a growing threat of famine, starvation and poverty in large areas of our planet.

The church likewise faces a major crisis in its mission and its vocational resources. It is becoming increasingly more difficult to proclaim the gospel in a secularized world. As the majority of the world population continues to shift toward the third world and the southern hemisphere, many of the more Eurocentric church attitudes, practices and disciplines seem to stand in the way of evangelization. In most parts of Europe and North America there are fewer and fewer priests to carry out the sacramental ministry of the church. In other areas of the world the widespread crisis of violence and oppression demands a gospel vision and a pastoral response, but divisions and priorities in the church often make such a response ineffective or even impossible.

What does partnership have to do with these global issues? In the face of so many other pressing problems, why should we be concerned about the need for women and men to minister together? What bearing does collaboration or mutuality have on the nuclear arms race, the breakdown of the family or the crisis in the church's mission to the world?

Some condemn the call to partnership between women and men as a dangerous threat to the church's tradition. The initial responses to the first draft of the U.S. bishops' letter on women reflect some of these sentiments. In essence, the more reactionary members of the church are criticizing the bishops for responding to a vocal minority who, in their opinion, are only a "fringe group" pushing a not-so-subtle form of feminism on the rest of the community. In their opinion, this movement is simply one more way in which the church is losing ground in maintaining its traditional values. This is not an unusual reaction to change or reform. It is often easier to agree that we are in crisis than to reach consensus on what we must do to respond to it.

All the same, we believe that the vision and practice of partnership between women and men is at the heart of the church's renewal. It is not peripheral but central to the crises that confront humankind and the church. The lack of such partnership has brought us close to the brink of disaster militarily, politically and ecologically. The lack of covenantal mutuality is contributing to the breakdown of marriage and family life. The lack of mutuality between women and men is blunting the church's task of evangelization. The lack of partnership has called into question the credibility of the church's teaching on international justice and peace. Not least of all, the lack of partnership has contributed significantly to the present crisis of vocational and ministerial resources.

The issue of women and men working together does not often appear in banner headlines in our diocesan newspapers or as the lead story in the evening news. But it is there beneath the surface, like an untapped source of energy or a chasm waiting to be bridged. Its absence shows in our domestic and global divisions; its potential is revealed in the healing and reconciling energy that, in some places, this movement is already bringing to our church and our world.

In short, we believe that the commitment to collaborate is one of the most important keys to our future together on this planet. The challenge of mutuality in ministry will be one of the most significant instruments in the church's renewal and in its ability to proclaim the gospel in our time.

The Historical Development of the Partnership Movement

When Pope John XXIII called the Second Vatican Council, he employed a metaphor that reflected his practical rootedness in everyday life. He spoke of the need to open the church's windows and let in some "fresh air." It is doubtful that Angelo Roncalli, even with his visionary sense of humor, anticipated the brisk breezes that were soon to begin blowing. The "sound of a rushing wind" (Acts 2:2) that came in the wake of Pope John's announcement has been interpreted in various ways, depending obviously on one's point of view. The more hopeful among us believed it was the sound of the Spirit ushering in a new Pentecost. Others felt that it was only a violent storm that would tear the church asunder. In either case, the winds continue to blow.

In the meantime, another metaphor might help us understand this time of transition in the church. Consider the image of an earthquake. It is a symbol with strong biblical roots and connotations. Isaiah and the other prophets spoke of the trembling of the earth as a sign of the new age (cf. Is 24:18-19; Joel 4:16). Matthew recalls that the earth was shaken to its depths at both the dying and rising of Jesus (27:54; 28:2).

In the words of Paul Tillich, we too are experiencing the "shaking of the foundations." This is an age of tremors, upheavals and aftershocks. When an earthquake rumbles through the countryside, it not only disturbs the office buildings and shopping malls, the homes and villages on the earth's surface; it also transforms the depths of the earth by rearranging its subterranean layers and geological formations. The most significant movement takes place beneath the surface.

A similar phenomenon occurs in human consciousness during a time of dramatic historical transition. In what can be described as a "psychic earthquake," human awareness undergoes a radical upheaval—a series of tremors that disturbs not only the surface of life and its arrangements, but that, more significantly, transforms the depths of our experience and the symbols with which we articulate it. This image of transformation at the depth, as well as the implication of perduring and radical upheaval makes an earthquake an apt way of thinking about our experience in the contemporary church.

The first tremors or signs of upheaval came with the changes of language and ritual that accompanied the liturgical reforms immediately in the wake of the Second

Vatican Council. Even then, in what might now be considered the optimistic phase of renewal, many experienced the challenge of change as a disturbing prospect. It is never easy to let go of long-cherished patterns of thought or behavior.

But these tremors were relatively mild compared to the stronger quakes that followed. The vision of Vatican II and the liturgical renewal sent shock waves rumbling through the church. The ground of comfortable familiarity fell out from under us. Everywhere we looked, the implications of change came up to confront us: the shattering of our monolithic structures; the collapse of scholastic categories as the exclusive tool of theology; the need to develop new instruments of human reflection; the challenging of celibacy as a "higher state of life" and the reaffirmation of marriage; the exodus of women and men from religious communities and priesthood; the dramatic decline of candidates for seminaries and novitiates.

Positive energies and new configurations of the church's terrain also came in the wake of change: the shift from Eurocentric structures toward the possibility of a world church; the growth of scriptural scholarship and the recovery of the Word; the burgeoning of new ministries in parish life; grassroots movements toward community, such as justice and peace ministries, Cursillo, Marriage Encounter, Renew, and the charismatic movement; a new emphasis on evangelization and the restoration of the catechumenate; the impact of liberation theology on Christian spirituality.

The tremors have not subsided. If anything, the most powerful quake is now moving, with full force and impact, through the church's life and vision. Its energy had stirred in the depths for a long time; its initial tremors came later than many of the earlier shifts in theology and structure. It came when many of us were not expecting it and in a form few of us anticipated. But its aftershocks and implications will be with us for a long time to come. We are speaking here of the rise of Christian feminism and the subsequent call to partnership between women and men in the church. This powerful force is both a challenge to and a reaffirmation of our Catholic tradition.

It is one thing to welcome liturgical and canonical changes in the church's pastoral practice. It is a far more threatening prospect to examine the hierarchical vision and the patriarchal stance that has functioned for centuries as the theological horizon of the church's life. This is not to suggest that there was a preconceived plan on the part of church leaders to deprive women of their role in the Christian community. Rather, we are speaking of a slowly evolving cultural bias, a psychic and historical "numbing" that, because it was practiced and theologically justified for centuries, gradually became an inherent component of church discipline, an attitude ingrained in the consciousness of believing men and women.

Again, the metaphor of an earthquake is an apt one. Over the centuries the practice and structures of sexism gradually hardened into place, like geological formations, layer upon layer, generation after generation, until the patriarchal terrain simply became a given; something one takes for granted, like the scriptural image of the "eternal hills," as though both the earth and the church's historical structures came in final form directly from the hand of God. Ironically, this is precisely the claim that some theologians, past and present, make in regard to the subservient role of women in the church.

As we have seen, the topic of women and their role in ministry emerged relatively late in the contemporary church's renewal. Except for a few visionary women and men who had been raising the question earlier, the majority of us arrived at this issue more slowly, either through personal and pastoral experience, or by following the trajectory of Vatican II to its theological conclusion. It was, in many instances, a gradual dawning of a deeply held truth that, like an earthquake in slow motion, began to rumble through our ecclesial awareness, bringing in its aftermath a diversity of personal responses and decisions.

For many women there was an initial stage of vague uneasiness, followed by a growing feeling of being disconnected from male structures of worship and leadership. This in turn led to emotions of anger and a sense of betrayal at the hands of the church they had loved and served. Some have given up and left the church altogether; others feel trapped by their circumstances and immobilized by their rage; still others have channeled their anger into action, as they continue to find or create experiences of collaboration and move the community forward toward authentic partnership.

There have been parallel experiences for men in the church. Some have reacted in fear and denial toward women who want to share in the work of ministry; others have adopted the rhetoric of collaboration without facing its deeper personal and ecclesial implications. For those men who were willing to pursue the consequences of Vatican II beyond the canonical and liturgical externals, this has been a time of self-questioning and risk, guilt and personal transformation. Those who have experienced the reality of collaboration know that the church cannot turn back.

Thus, for the entire church the issue of women and men as partners in the Christian community has become a turning point of decision and direction. It is no longer possible to detach ourselves from the deeper implications of renewal. What began as *aggiornamento*—updating—has become a profound call to conversion. In the '60s we rearranged the furniture in the church. In the '70s we gave theological reasons for this new configuration. In the '80s we have discovered that the whole house needs renovating. It is no longer a case of updating various liturgical rituals or canonical structures; it is no longer as simple as rethinking our methods of catechesis or evangelization. As we approach the beginning of the third millennium of Christianity, the very message and mission of the gospel needs reformulation and re-enfleshment.

The Implications of Partnership for the Wider Church

A transformation in Christian self-understanding arises initially in the consciousness of individuals and in the experience of intentional communities of faith. But the energy of change cannot be limited to these circles of life. Eventually it begins to shake the foundations of the church as an institution as well; it affects the leaders who carry the responsibility for articulating the institution's vision and *ethos*. The struggle and searching, the quiet anguish of individuals as they embrace the implications of their vision, has an impact on the wider community and creates a parallel challenge in the institutional leadership.

In theological language we refer to this phenomenon as the *sensus fidelium*—that instinct of prayerful faith in the Body of Christ that, in key moments in the church's history, is guided by the Holy Spirit. This ground swell of experience, prayer and reflection cannot be ignored indefinitely by those who exercise leadership, nor can it be easily neutralized by official rhetoric. In the end, the church as an institution must wrestle with the same fundamental issues with which each of its members and ministers struggles. The whole church is challenged to hear the Word and to keep it, to see the vision and interpret it (Jer 1:11-13).

Thus, in the current tensions that surround the question of women and men in ministry, there is a certain irony of the Spirit at work. In a striking manner the institutional church is being confronted with the consequences of its own envisioning process, invited to listen to a "play-back" of its teachings as they have been enfleshed in the lives of believers who take seriously Vatican II's emphasis on the dignity of the human person and the gospel call to equality. What the teaching church has articulated in its encyclicals and proclaimed in the council documents, the ministers and communities of faith are attempting to live out on the local level.

As early as 1963, when Pope John XXIII wrote *Pacem in Terris*, the church was already expressing its commitment to work toward greater mutuality between women and men in society. John XXIII pointed to three important "signs of the times" that he wished to address in his letter: 1) the emancipation of the worker; 2) the emergence of the developing nations; and 3) the increasing participation of women in public life. Commenting on the last of these issues, John makes this remarkable statement: "Women are gaining an increasing awareness of their natural dignity. Far from being content with a purely passive role or allowing themselves to be regarded as a kind of instrument, they are demanding both in domestic and in public life the rights and duties which belong to them as human persons" (#41).

Only two years later, after the death of John XXIII and toward the end of the Second Vatican Council, the "Pastoral Constitution on the Role of the Church in the Modern World" (*Gaudium et Spes*), declared that "with respect to the fundamental rights of the human person, every type of discrimination, whether social or cultural, whether based on sex, race, color, social condition, language, or religion, is to be overcome and eradicated as contrary to God's intent" (#29).

The role of women and their equality may have emerged as an issue relatively late in the renewal process, but it did so in direct continuity with the social encyclicals of this century, the vision of Vatican II, and many of the homilies that Pope Paul VI and John Paul II have delivered in their travels to various parts of the world.

What is at stake, therefore, is the institutional church's response to its own vision. What is the deeper spirit of the Second Vatican Council? How are we to read its documents? Was it intended to be a beacon or a boundary? Is it a starting point for renewal or a still-born vision that can be reduced to the safe parameters of canonical legislation?

The challenge of partnership between women and men may well be the primary arena in which these questions will be answered. Far from being the agenda of a "fringe group" in the Christian community, it is rather the testing ground of the church's authenticity. Despite the pronouncements and fears of some church leaders, the question of women in the church and their call to ministerial partnership is not an issue that will quietly disappear. It is here to stay. It is, in fact, rapidly becoming one of the central issues of pastoral and ecclesial theology. For some this may be a threatening reality, but in the long run, it may well be a sign of the Spirit at work in history.

Toward a More Catholic Church

Vatican II became the launching pad for a new energy in the church. It affirmed the movement toward greater expansiveness and global inclusiveness. It was the first visible sign, Karl Rahner tells us, that we are breaking out of a Eurocentric framework toward a more global perspective. This transition carries with it the possibility of becoming more truly "catholic," in the broad meaning of a world-church, rather than "Roman" in the more narrow cultural sense. At the Second Vatican Council, for the first time in history, large numbers of bishops from the Third World made their perspective known. At the extraordinary synod of bishops in 1985, 60 percent of the episcopal delegates were from developing countries.

This movement toward cultural diversity is a sign of great vitality in the church, but it highlights even more the significant lack of inclusiveness and collaboration on other levels. The church may indeed be embracing the riches of other cultures, but at the level of its institutional leadership it is still predominantly patriarchal in its perspective. Even as the church reaches out to dialogue with and learn from other cultures, it continues to exclude more than half of its members from realizing the full potential of their baptismal dignity.

By almost everyone's standards, the Second Vatican Council is the historical turning point for the church in the 20th century. But no women were present at or participating in the Second Vatican Council. The extraordinary synod of 1985, despite initial fears, reaffirmed the fundamental vision of Vatican II. No women participated in that synod, not even among the Protestant and Orthodox observers. No women have a deliberative voice at the meetings of the United States Conference of Catholic

Bishops; no women have leadership positions in the curial offices of the Vatican. And yet, it is safe to assume that the majority of actual ministry in the church—the teaching, healing, nurturing, and forming of communities of faith—is carried out by women. Furthermore, lay men are often as ignored as women in a church where ordained, celibate males are the only ones who have access to sacramental leadership and decision-making power. Today the institutional church itself, as much as the world to which it preaches, stands challenged by the gospel and its implications.

But the church's institutional leadership is not alone. We are all challenged to a deeper conversion and a more authentic way of life. The issues that face us in today's church are deeper than our need to confront destructive forms of patriarchy. The gospel and the current teaching of the church both challenge us to come to grips with oppression and elitism wherever it is encountered. But that isn't enough. The issue is more than hierarchical structures and sexism. It is even greater than the emergence of women's self-awareness. In the end, we are challenged to move beyond sexism to mutuality, beyond division to unity, beyond bitterness to reconciliation, beyond competition to collaboration. We are called, in short, to journey toward partnership.

2
It Is Not Good to Be Alone
The Hebrew Roots of Partnership

Partnership is not a new idea. It is not one more contemporary fad that will disappear with time. Male-female partnership is as old as the ancient Hebrew poets who, inspired by the Spirit of God, crafted images and words to describe the mystery of creation.

To say that God created is to say that God had a vision, a vision shaped by a purpose and permeated with divine energy. It was a colorful vision of blue water and red sunsets, a vision as gentle as spring and as serious as winter. It was a vision of animals raising their young in the shadow of seed bearing trees. It was, above all, a relational vision bursting with the sights and sounds and smells and flavors of a universe at peace with itself.

It was a vision of a woman and a man, naked before each other, transparent to the core of their being, as they stood eager for friendship and ready to share the joy of tending the earth. More than being representative of a model "first couple," or a prototype of sexual relationships, this man and woman stand for all of us. They represent every woman and every man in their primordial

31

call to equality and mutuality. They stand as a beacon of God's creative intention: that humankind is best imaged as male and female in a shared covenant of mutuality.

At the heart of God's creative intention, therefore, is the call to *partnership*. Partnership is the persistent theme that weaves the divine dream together. The roots of partnership are as deep as the soil and as expansive as the skies. Although given fullest expression in the woman and the man, some dimension of partnership—that fundamental and holy standing together—is at the heart of all that God made.

In the Hebrew world-view, heaven and earth were the two great partners of the universe, partners whose mutual energies nourished and housed all living things, from the smallest of plants to the largest of creatures. The seas and the dry land were rhythmic partners that stayed in constant touch, ebbing and flowing against each other, yet not violating each others' space. They fed and watered God's creatures, each of whom needed a balance of their abundant resources. The sun and the moon, partners of time and shared guardians of the seasons, were the givers of light and darkness in right measure. Fruit trees and plants, all kinds of vegetation were invited to share their seed, to need each other so profoundly that their very existence would depend upon their interdependence. Living creatures, sea serpents and fishes, birds and cattle, all manner of wild animals and beasts, none were able to live without each other. To survive and grow, they needed to share the gifts of creation. In God's plan, life cannot be born of isolation.

And finally, the woman and the man were also invited into a partnership at once compelling and sacred. The God of creativity filled them with a powerful passion for partnership, an urgent desire to move toward each other. The capacity for reproductive union, assigned to the plant and animal world, was taken a further step with the woman and the man. The fundamental basis of their joining would not rest on a pelvic urge or a mating instinct. Theirs would be a kind of knowing that would carry them through their flesh and beyond it to the depth of their innermost dreams and feelings. They would share so much more than their reproductive energy. They would stand face to face, hand in hand, united in myriad forms of friendship, before each other and before the earth.

Let Us Make Humankind

In the creation of the woman and the man, the notion of partnership in Genesis 1 assumes its most profound meaning:

> God said, "Let us make humankind
> in our own image,
> in the likeness of ourselves,...."
> (cf. Gn 1:26).

Let *us* make. In *our own*. Of *ourselves*. God, in a rare portrayal of acting in the plural, assumes a stance of partnership in the very act of creating humanity. Mutuality gives birth to itself.

Here, the priestly author uses the plural term, *elohim,* to refer to God. Later spiritual writers would read this passage from their theological perspective and cite "them" as evidence for a trinity of persons in the Godhead. The literary style hints of a deeper theological reality: God exists and acts not in a stance of isolation but of union, a kind of union that has always been considered an incomprehensible mystery.

In a world where countless generations have grown up familiar with warfare, boundary disputes and racial hatred, is it any wonder that we must consider powerful and consistent union among persons to be a mystery? After centuries of suspicion, competition and rivalry, would not total mutuality stand out as a marvel to us? Our usual ways of relating to each other are charged with militarism, racism, classism and sexism. Such realities as union and partnership stand in stark contrast to our experience, indeed to the very ethic of nationalism on which our globe precariously rests. Perhaps we need to assign the label "mystery" to anything that is not in our repertory of behaviors.

A union of persons in God may be incomprehensible to us not because it is beyond our human capacity to understand but because it is beyond our willingness to put it into practice. Do the plural referents to God tease us with a mystery we can never hope to grasp, or do they offer us a model we must strive to enflesh?

Let us. In our own. Of ourselves. Rhetoric or revelation? Mystery or mandate?

If we dismiss the language as merely rhetorical, having no particular revelatory significance, we lose something of the rich imagery in the text. If we acknowledge that the literary style points to something (i.e. the Trinity), but call it a mystery, it loses much of its nearness to us. It can remain in the remote world of speculative theology and never touch our lives. Rather than becoming a model for all human relationships, God as "communion of persons" can be carefully defined in theology textbooks, preserved from error and kept safe from those who want to get too familiar with divine Truth.

But if we savor the poetry, if we let the imagery gently flow through us, not just into our minds so that we can grasp it intellectually, but into our flesh so we can feel it, the simple truth of the partnership vision will overwhelm us. There is something so inherently other-orienting in the divine that God cannot be thought of as solitary. There is such intense mutuality, such all consuming union, that the divine reality cannot be fully expressed only in the singular. The essence of partnership is contained in the very image of God.

Creation is the extension of divine partnership into the universe and into humanity. This same relational God places a hunger for union, a drive toward mutuality in the woman and the man. They carry within their natures a fundamental urge toward partnering. Partnership describes their nature and foretells their destiny.

In God's Image: The Priestly Account of Partnership

Humanity finds its origins in a God who images divinity through creation. What does this imply about

God's identity? In what ways do women and men reflect God? What does it mean to be created in God's image? Is this just another literary device, or does it embody some deeper truth?

In the past, some spiritual writers have suggested that the likeness humanity bears to God lies in the realm of the spirit or soul. But the concept of a spiritual soul as distinct from the body would have been foreign to the Hebrew mentality. When the writings of Genesis were taking shape, the Jewish people understood the human person to be one whole entity, not divided into body and soul. The assumption that men and women are like God only in some spiritual way or in the soul is a later interpretation that finds its origins in Greek philosophy. We must look for the theological meaning of humanity's likeness to God in a way that fits with the Hebrew poet's understanding and use of language:

> And God created humankind in his image,
> in the image of God he created him;
> male and female he created them
> (cf. Gn 1:27).

The Hebrew *demuth* (likeness) literally means "resemblance." It has connotations of a blueprint or an exact copy, something that mirrors another reality quite exactly. The word *selem* (image) implies a sculpted statue (as in the Greek *eikon*). Such a statue is not simply a semblance but an exact visual reproduction, a surrogate of the otherwise unseen reality (Vawter, p.55).

The Israelites were forbidden to make images of the diety, but the same prohibition was obviously not binding on God. Presumably, God is in the position to know enough about divinity to create a likeness that conforms closely to divine reality. This is exactly what the sacred author suggests. If we move the words of the poetry around to reflect the Hebrew style of writing, this becomes more clear:

> And God created humankind *in his image.*
> *in-the-image* of God created he him;
> *male and female* created he them
> (cf. Gn 1:27).

This verse is a metaphor which contains two types of parallelism. Lines one and two reflect inverted parallelism, while lines two and three contain straight parallelism. The word *image* is the focus of these poetic lines. The repetition of this word twice in the first two lines underscores its importance in the action. The meaning of "image of God" is revealed in the third line. "Clearly, 'male and female' correspond structurally to 'the image of God,'..." (Trible, p.17). In the metaphor, a lesser known thing, "image of God," is compared to a greater known thing, "male and female," for the purpose of shedding light on both of them. The metaphor thus compares likenesses and in so doing, challenges us to a deeper understanding of the "image of God." Poetry is not intended to answer our questions. It gives us images, not definitions. "Poetry invites, but does not compel, insight" (Trible, p.16).

In the image of God. Male and female. The invitation is clearly there to make some association between the two. Male and female have something to tell us about the image of God. And the image of God has something to tell us about male and female.

There is something so vital about maleness and femaleness that it becomes, for the priestly poet, the primary way in which humanity's identity is described. Male and female are poised together at humanity's infancy in a stance of partnership, a partnership that reflects God's very selfhood. They stand as equals, created simultaneously, both contributing to the fundamental definition of what it means to be human. Without either of them, humanity would lose something vital to its identity. So would the image of God.

As the poetry unfolds, both the male and the female are given the resources of the earth. Both share dominion. God speaks to both of them at the same time, giving each the same message. No separate roles are assigned. Their only distinctions lie in their sexuality. God does not assign different sets of responsibilities, different degrees of authority, or different capacities to image God.

Neither the male nor the female have dominion over each other; they share it. In other words, dominion can only be properly exercised by both of them in mutual cooperation with each other. God speaks only when both of them are in union with each other. God's word is not spoken to one without the other. Partnership is a vital component for the reception and interpretation of God's word. Neither male alone nor female alone can presume to be representative of humanity—or of God.

The image of God. Male and female. The metaphor could not be more compelling. It invites us to see the woman and the man in a playful encounter with divinity and to watch them emerge imbued with God's aura. As they dance around God's image, they leave something of their unique essence upon an amazingly receptive God, a God who takes delight in viewing the woman and the man as icons of the divine.

This is biblical partnership: to be unique and separate, yet enfolded in another's reality; to be whole in oneself, yet in need of the other to reflect one's reality. Women and men must be that for each other and for God.

The Adam and Eve Story: The Yahwist Account of Partnership

An earlier Hebrew poet told a different story of beginnings. In Genesis 2, with the familiar "Adam and Eve" story, the writer begins with the creation of what appears to be a single creature, *"ha-'adam,"* and traces its development into male and female. At first glance, Genesis 2 sounds like a story totally different from Genesis 1. The stories are distinct, but if we look more deeply we will discover the same underlying theme: Common soil and holy breath are united. Divinity and humanity mingle. Creation begins in partnership and flourishes in mutuality.

Almost since commentators began exacting meaning from the creation account in Genesis 2, the story has suffered misinterpretation. The partnership theme, so prominent in these verses, has usually been read from a patriarchal perspective. Trible has noted that the misogynous reading of the "Adam and Eve" story has, over the centuries, acquired a status of canonicity (Trible, p. 73). She offers an impressive list of specific "beliefs" derived from the innacurate readings. All of them have been used to assert male superiority and female subordination as the will of God:

—— A male God creates man first (2:7) and woman last (2:22).

—— First means superior and last means inferior or subordinate.

—— Woman is created for the sake of man—a helpmate to cure his loneliness (2:18-23).

—— Woman is the rib of man, dependent on him for life (2:21-22).

—— Taken from the rib of man, woman has a derivative, not an autonomous existence (2:23).

—— Man names woman (2:23) and thus has power over her.

—— Woman tempted man; she is responsible for sin in the world (3:6).

—— Woman is cursed by pain in childbirth (3:16); bearing children becomes the way woman can redeem herself.

—— God gives man the right to rule over woman (3:16).

While none of these statements is accurate, and most of them are not even present in the story, many Christians would find them so familiar as to believe that they come from the very lips of God. Fundamentalists anxious to maintain the subordination of women continue to expound these distortions. Using God's word on partnership as a vehicle to oppress women represents a curious twist of religious behavior.

Genesis 2 is not a story about a man who is created by God and then is later given a woman to meet his needs and raise his children. It is the story of partnership offered as an ideal, but tragically not achieved.

A New Reading of the Adam and Eve Story

Yahweh God fashioned *man* of dust from the soil. Then he breathed into *his* nostrils a breath of life, and thus *man* became a living *being*. This traditional translation of Genesis 2:7, found in one form or another in most of our bibles, will sound familiar—for many, familiar enough to have long ago been committed to memory. There, in the recesses of our minds it influences our world-view, molding images of ourselves and of the women and men of our lives. In a subtle, almost subconscious manner, the male use of language shapes our beliefs and influences our behavior.

Ironically, scripture scholars have known for several decades that the words in italics have been incorrectly translated. Yet, because many of them believe that changing familiar translations would be threatening to the faithful, the story continues to to be translated as it has in the past. Only in the footnotes of some editions of the bible, do we see some of the italicized words translated correctly.

How would this translation look if we used the tools of scripture scholarship? We can begin by transliterating the italicized words into their original language:

> Then Yahweh God formed *ha-'adam*
> of dust from *ha-'adama*
> and breathed into its nostrils the breath of life,
> and *ha-'adam* became a living *nephesh*.

A closer look at each of the italicized words will give us a clue to the meaning of the poetry and the divine truth which it contains:

adama	*earth*
adam	*earth creature*
ha	*the*

As can be seen, the words *adama* and *adam* represent a pun, a playful exchange of images. The Hebrew *ha* is simply the definite article. Used in connection with both *adama* and *adam,* it indicates that we are dealing in each instance with a noun, not a particular person by the name of Adam. When we replace the original Hebrew words with their correct translations, a very different story emerges:

> Then Yahweh God formed *the earth creature*
> of dust from *the earth*
> and breathed into *its* nostrils the breath of life
> and *the earth creature* became a living *nephesh*.

The Hebrew *nephesh* is a difficult word to translate since it has no exact English equivalent. It has connotations of total selfhood. Yet, here in the story its usage suggests a gradually unfolding selfhood, one that cannot be assumed as completed until we are told that it is finished. The *earth creature* is in process and continues to take shape throughout the story.

How, then, are we to interpret the creation process of Genesis 2? If God is not making the first man, just what is happening? And what does it have to do with partnership?

Imagine some loose, dry soil. Imagine it to be quite still and seemingly inert. Then picture breath beginning to blow lightly over the soil until the particles begin to move. Gradually, as the warm breath moves over the soil, both begin to swirl into each other, to come alive.

This image of swirling soil is the earth creature at the beginning moments of creation. But the breath that awakens the soil is not just any breath. It is divine breath, God's breath. Dusty earth is joined by holy breath and mystery unfolds. God's life mingles with the soil and evokes a creature at once earthy and divine. It is a powerful image!

If this creature is to become, as the Yahwist poet indicates, the source of all humanity, then its origins have something to say about ours. In a biblical sense, we all hold the earth creature within our nature. Like it, we are a wondrous combination of dusty earth and divine breath. We are indeed holy ground. We have been quickened by the very breath of the divine and the earth is truly our mother.

Once the dust has been penetrated by God's life-giving breath, the process of humanity's journey toward full selfhood (*nephesh*) has begun. The word *process* is especially important in this context. As we read the earth creature's story, we may not assume anything we have not yet been told. The Hebrew writer is a poet, not a reporter. He is more interested in creating an experience for us than in giving us raw facts. To experience revealed truth in the poetry, we must proceed at the poet's pace, not second guessing, not with prior assumptions, but with hearts open to the surprise of the Spirit.

As we enter again into the earth creature's development, we know only a few things. First, the earth creature (*ha-'adam*) is neither a particular person, nor a typical person, but is, at this stage, simply a combination of dust and breath—a creature taken from the earth and not yet completed. It is a passive creature, being acted upon by God, and not yet capable of initiating action on its own. Its only capacity, at this point, is the capacity to receive breath. God is its breather, sustaining each moment of its existence.

Second, this earth creature is sexually undifferentiated. Since sexuality is not created until much later in the story, we cannot assume that the earth creature posesses it here. *Ha-'adam* is therefore neither male nor female. It can in no way be construed to be the first male without doing violence to the poet's intention.

As the story continues, *ha-'adam* moves from a passive creature located in a garden to an active worker, namer, and decision maker:

> And Yahweh God took *ha-'adam*
> and put it in the garden of Eden
> to till (*'bd*) it and to keep (*smr*) it
> (cf. Gn 2:17).

In this part of the poetry, we are told that the earth creature is responsible for the care of the garden. The Hebrew words *'bd* (till) and *smr* (keep) actually mean to serve and to protect. They connote reverence toward the earth. The earth creature is now no longer a passive recipient of God's energizing breath; rather, it must use its energy and breath on behalf of the earth.

As the story unfolds, the earth creature is given instructions from God:

> You may eat indeed of all the trees in the garden. Nevertheless of the tree of knowledge of good and evil you are not to eat,...
> (Gn 2:16).

We can now conclude that the earth creature can hear, think and make choices. In addition to hearing, other senses appear. It can see the plants and trees, and can taste their fruits. It attains some form of mobility. Sexuality, however, has still not been assigned. At this point in the story the earth creature remains neuter.

The picture that emerges is one of a benevolent creature, who works, listens to God, and experiences some enjoyment in the many delights of the garden. But something is missing. The earth creature is still too limited. It has not yet spoken. And we are given a hint that it is lonely.

God assesses this plight of the earth creature and senses a need for further intervention. Before the earth creature can continue in its journey toward full selfhood, something more is needed, something vital to its completion. At this point in the story God makes a dramatic announcement—a proclamation that will reverberate down through the centuries and echo in the heart of humanity for all time:

> It is not good
> for *ha-'adam* to be alone.

Continuing to exist in the state of isolation is not according to God's plan for the earth creature. It is not good. Being existentially alone is not life-sustaining. A perpetual condition of loneliness is destructive. It keeps the earth creature frozen in a state of incompleteness. Its continued development demands companionship.

And Yahweh God said,
It is not good for *ha-'adam* to be alone.
I will make for it an *ezer k negdo*
(cf. Gn 2:18-19).

God proposes *ezer k negdo* as a solution for the earth creature's loneliness. The Hebrew *ezer* is usually translated helper or helpmate—words that imply assistance to someone in a position of superiority. Actually, these translations are unfortunate, both because they miss the full import of the meaning of *ezer*, and also because they serve to perpetuate the sterotype that woman was created to be a helper (hence, a subordinate) to man.

Ezer actually means a companion. In no way does it imply inferiority. In fact, only true equals can be genuine companions for one another. The Hebrew *ezer* is used elsewhere in the Old Testament to refer to God: "Our soul awaits Yahweh, he is our *ezer* and shield" (cf. Ps 33:20). The companionship that will heal the isolation of the earth creature is comparable to that offered by God to creatures.

The accompanying phrase, *k negdo,* further qualifies and describes the kind of companionship the earth creature will receive. The phrase means "corresponding to it." It implies full equality, mutuality and identity.

Ezer k negdo. A companion corresponding to it. Essential for support. Vital for completion. There could be no stronger mandate for partnership. Creation is unfinished. Humanity is incomplete until the condition of *ezer k negdo* is established.

The Tardemah Experience

What follows is a process some scholars have referred to as divine trial and error. In an effort to secure a companion for the lonely earth creature, God fashions a variety of animals and birds and brings them to it. The still sexually undifferentiated earth creature receives and names each of them, but none of the feathered or furry creatures alleviates *ha-'adam's* persistent sense of isolation. We are simply told:

> . . . But as for *ha-'adam,*
> it did not find a companion
> corresponding to itself
> > (cf. Gn 2:20-21).

This solitary situation cannot go on. It is not God's intention that the earth creature continue to exist without companionship. Immediately, God intervenes, only this time the action is decisive and complete:

> And Yahweh God
> caused a *tardemah* to fall upon *ha-'adam*
> and while it slept,
> > took one of its ribs
> > and closed up flesh in that spot
> > > (cf. Gn 2:21-22).

How does *ezer k negdo* come into being? How is the earth creature suddenly moved from the stance of isolation to the stance of partnership? The answer is *tardemah*. This Hebrew word is usually translated "deep sleep." It is a word rarely used in the Old Testament writings and indicates more than routine sound slumber. Typically, its use is associated with an important activity initiated by God. For example, the deep sleep (*tardemah*) of Abram signals the making of the covenant (Gn 15:12).

For the earth creature, *tardemah* provides the poet's explanation of the way in which partnership comes about. In some mysterious and highly significant way, God causes the earth creature to undergo an awesome transformation quite beyond our ability to understand or explain. The *tardemah* experience is so powerful that the very flesh of the neuter earth creature is forever altered. *Ha-'adam* emerges as male and female *(ish* and *ishshah)* as a result of God's transforming action. From this point in the narrative, *ha-'adam* is no longer the *ha-'adam* we met in the beginning, but is rather a different creature. He has sexuality. He is male. And most spectacular of all, he is no longer alone. An identical companion that conforms exactly to his nature has been found! For the first time, the now transformed *ha-'adam* speaks directly and heralds the cry of biblical partnership:

> This at last is bone from my bones
> and flesh of my flesh
> (Gn 2:23).

Only after the *tardemah* experience are sexual identities used in the story. Male and female emerge together out of the one flesh of the earth creature. They are flesh of each other's flesh, companions whose identity is shared by a common humanity, yet made distinctive and unique by separate sexualities.

Ezer k negdo, the experience of companionship that could alleviate destructive isolation, was not found among the animals. Nor was it found in the separate and solitary toil of the earth creature. *Ezer k negdo* becomes a reality only when *ha-'adam*, the unfinished earth creature, emerges into male and female. Human sexuality makes possible the experience of mutuality and companionship that the asexual being can never know. The creation of human sexuality represents the culminating high point of the story. It signals movement from isolation to community. And, for the first time in the story, humanity has the ability to speak. The potential for full self-expression comes in the context of partnership. "This one at last!" Humanity's first words express its destiny—a destiny directed toward relationship, a destiny that signals mutuality as humanity's ultimate source of excitement. Sexuality makes intimacy possible for humanity.

In both creation accounts of Genesis, the story ends with the man and the woman standing in partnership. This primordial partnership is the oldest of visions, the best of God's dreams. It was to serve as a witness, a beacon for all of creation. It was to be a reminder that life is best served by mutuality, that peace is best promoted by relationships. It was a call to all people for all time to enter into partnership with each other and with the earth. Only in partnership can women and men stroll unashamed in the cool of the afternoon with their God.

The Hebrew authors describe creation as only poets can—with vivid images and vast ideals. They wanted to say, as emphatically as they could, that male-female partnership was fundamental to God's creative intention and foundational to life. They wanted readers through the ages to get caught up in the images of inter-dependence and to feel the excitement of humanity's first cry: "This at last is bone from my bone and flesh of my flesh." Someone in my world shares my skin, some-one else in the garden understands the joy and burden of tending the earth, someone else fashioned by a God who thought that persistent loneliness was not a good idea. This one at last!

3
The Fall
The Rupture of Partnership

If the Hebrew poets had been inclined to separate theology from life, the "Adam and Eve story" might have ended with the creation of woman and man. The two could have been left to wander in their garden, an idyllic reminder of God's gracious role in humanity's beginnings. Their fate unknown and its outcome unnecessary, they would have stood frozen in time, adequate proof of God's creative power.

But the authors of Genesis were not content to offer literary answers to the "how did we get here" question. Social critics as well as poets, theologians connected to life in the real world, they turned their attention to even more pressing concerns. Now that we are here, enfleshed as males and females, how are we to be with one another? Does the poetry of creation have anything to say to the reality of living?

This one at last! It was not just a romantic ending to a biblical fairy tale. Nor was it a clever conclusion to an Old Testament apologetic, content to provide answers but devoid of any implications for the future. This one at last! It was an invitation more than a conclusion. It was a new theological moment, the proclamation of a vision that was to guide women and men past the loneliness of isolation to the energizing place of shared dreams and mutual pursuits.

Yet, as profoundly as the sacred authors believed that partnership lay at the heart of God's good creation, and that its call was deeply embedded in all creatures, they saw a different reality being lived in their time. They saw a world where partnership had been fractured and where mutuality was only a dim memory of a far away garden. They saw a religious structure open only to males and a society in which women were considered the property of fathers and husbands. Clearly, the world reality did not conform to the partnership vision. This broken state of humankind demanded an explanation. Why were women and men no longer expressing the goodness of being flesh of each other's flesh, bone of each other's bone? Why had the primordial excitement of mutuality died?

The Hebrew poets faced a monumental task. They had to present the vision of mutuality with an intensity and fire worthy of God's word, while at the same time explaining why it was not being enfleshed in the lives of the women and men of their day. Finally, they had to offer a promise of hope in the eventual restoration of partnership. As complicated as this task was, the poets of the Hebrew scriptures accomplished it with all of the color of an artist's palette and the passion of a great composer.

The poetry of the Hebrew scriptures unfolds like a well orchestrated symphony. First, there is the vision of mutuality, the portrayal of life in the garden. Then, there is the tragedy of the vision being lost and the expulsion from the garden. In the final movement, the author of the Song of Songs, writing at a different time but hearing the same holy music, offers hope in the eventual restoration of God's dream for women and men. In the garden. Out of the garden. The garden restored. The composition represents all of the movements of life: innocence, loss, restoration.

Life in the Garden: The Birth of Mutuality

In the early moments in the garden, immediately after the emergence of the male and female, we glimpse the essence of mutuality. It is found in a simple, straightforward description of the original state of the pair. It is expressed in their primordial stance toward each other: "Now both of them were naked. . . but they felt no shame in front of each other. . ." (Gn 2:25).

Naked and without shame. Are we to assume literal nudity and smile gently at the childlike existence of the first pair, or do these words invite deeper contemplation? If we argue for a literal interpretation, then this part of the story has little more to say to us. It offers no challenge for today, since it could hardly be argued that a return to the state of physical nakedness is part of God's intention for all humanity.

But if we believe that a deeper theological truth lies behind the literal meaning of these words, then we can assume that the nakedness of the primordial couple involved something more than the absence of fig leaves.

To be physically naked is to have one's body uncovered. But there are many forms of nakedness. We can be "uncovered" or "naked" emotionally by letting our feelings show, by refusing to hide anger, hurt, loneliness, excitement or love.

We can be psychologically naked by engaging in self-disclosure, by being vulnerable, by letting someone else know who we are at the deepest level of our lives.

We can be radically naked to self, totally honest and willing to look at all dimensions of our reality and experience. Accurate self-knowledge is usually the result of this type of nakedness.

Naked and *without shame*. The Hebrew word *bosh* is translated "ashamed." It literally means to "become pale" in relationship to another. It describes a situation in which a person experiences diminishment at the hands of another. In our day, we can say that any form of behavior that causes a person to feel bad about himself or herself, to be demeaned or abused emotionally or physically, is an experience of Hebrew "boshness."

At the dawn of creation, the Hebrew author is making an emphatic point. When the woman and the man first stood before each other, neither was diminished in relationship to the other. The existence of the one in no way caused the other to feel insignificant. This was God's intention. This reality is essential to the theological perspective of Genesis 2, and provides us with the central truth about mutuality. Whatever else might be said about it, mutuality is, in essence, the life-giving experience of feeling valued in relationship to another.

As the story unfolds, it becomes clear that the woman and the man were entirely comfortable with the mutuality they experienced. They felt no need to put the other down, to control the other, or to shine at the other's expense. We are speaking here about something more than an early version of the Equal Rights Amendment. Biblical nakedness goes beyond fairness in relationships. The absence of diminishment does not simply mean that the pair stood on the same rung of the Israelite ladder of success.

They were *naked*. Their original state was that of transparency and vulnerability in relationship to each other. They could stand before each other as they were, with nothing to hide. They could share their deepest secrets without fear of ridicule. They could face each other honestly and know they would not lose respect or love. If we accept only a literal interpretation of this passage, we will miss the deeper meaning of this primordial nakedness. We will be left with the impression that it is a statement about clothing rather than being.

This one at last? Partnership? Mutuality? What happened to God's creative intention for women and men? What went wrong? The poets of Genesis took great pains to describe the simultaneous and equal creation of male and female. They also took care to describe the radical nakedness that enveloped the first couple. But when the poets turned their attention to their own times, they did not see male-female mutuality. A radically different reality stared back at them: patriarchy, slavery, blood taboos, women forbidden a part in male rituals. It was a far cry from the vision. Such a distance from God's dream. How could they explain it? What would God say?

Outside the Garden: The Failure of Mutuality

There had been a "fall," the author of Genesis 2 explained. The vision stood. But the woman and the man had failed it. There had been a grasp for power, a desire for independent self-fulfillment. The urge for easy achievement was stronger than the willingness to accept the limitations of mutuality. The promise of power seemed to outweigh the risks of vulnerability.

And then the woman and the man experienced what all power seekers come to know:

—— the need to hide from each other.

—— the need to cover up.

—— the need to blame.

—— the need to run from mutuality and escape into the private world of self preservation.

—— the need to give excuses for the escape, even to God.

The story of the fall is a powerful image that speaks to all ages of a lost vision. Its message is clear. The fall is not a simple tumble out of God's favor for two tragic, weak-willed figures of the past. It is not just an isolated act of disobedience made historic by Old Testament poetry. Nor can it be easily dismissed from serious spirituality as a mythical tale borrowed from pagan literature. Claiming it to be a literal bite of a forbidden fruit provides biblical justification for sexism, conveniently making women the scapegoat for societal ills. Emphasizing it only as a sin of pride effectively takes the focus off the deeper meaning of the fall—the failure of mutuality— and thus offers no challenge to restore partnership among males and females in our day.

The fall is a symbol, a strong and tragic image of the effects of ruptured partnership, of God's dream gone awry. The biblical story gives perspective to a reality that is as actual today as it was then:

—— Full partnership between women and men is

fundamental to God's creative intention and a foundation of biblical spirituality.

—— Central to the vision of male-female partnership is a parallel call to partnership with the earth and the rest of the universe.

—— The earth and her children become victims when partnership ruptures. When women and men fall out of mutuality, they take all of creation with them. The vision grows dim.

The story tells us that the woman and the man experienced the earth as an enemy when they became enemies to each other. They saw the once nourishing plants as brambles and thistles. The soil fought the plow. Birth was painful. And so was life. Killing began. Violence spread.

What had once been a tranquil state of mutual delight and shared responsibility suddenly changed into a dark world of separation and shame. The poetry of Genesis offers us a theological message about this tragic state of affairs:

> But Yahweh God called to the man.
> "Where are you?" he asked.
> "I heard the sound of you in the garden;"
> he replied "I was afraid"
>   because I was naked, so I hid."
> "Who told you that you were naked?"
>   (Gn 3:9-11).

There is almost a sense of surprise on the part of God that the man was aware of his nakedness. Nakedness, after all, was part of the divine plan for the man and the woman. It should not be cause for discomfort, much less hiding. But by now, the reversal of God's order had taken place. Nakedness had changed from being a state of delight to an occasion for hiding. The first and most paralyzing result of the fall was the advent of shame. No longer could the man and the woman be vulnerable and open with one another. No longer would the thought of self-discovery bring joy. Instead, hiding replaced openness. Delight in nakedness gave way to fear. Patriarchy

had begun to sink its roots into human consciousness.
Sexism would soon follow.

The Fall: Implications for Our Time

In the biblical image of hiding the full implications of
the fall become clear. When women and men turn to separate pursuits, when they exchange vulnerability for
protection, the care of the earth is no longer a shared priority. When they prefer blaming to reconciling, competing to collaborating, then something fundamental to
global peace is lost.

Today, like the Israelite poets and prophets of old, we
live in a world of ruptured partnership. The signs are all
around us: Lonely women and men who can't find intimacy in their lives; the suspicion with which same-sex
friendships are viewed; the ways in which sexual behavior is used as a weapon of violence instead of a celebration of union.

Our broken way of relating on an interpersonal level
is, in turn, passed on to the international scene. The little
quarrels in our living rooms become a way of life in the
larger world. Nation battles nation as our ability to make
bombs surpasses our capacity to make conversation
with our enemies. Government leaders who dismiss
trust as naive may have learned mistrust from the dysfunctional family interactions of their childhoods. The
parents who are unable to experience genuine mutuality
pass this lack of connection on to their unsuspecting
children. A child who grows up in an environment where
arguments are more common than sharing, and where
insults replace communication, learns the basic lessons
of a war-torn environment: Above all else, protect your-
self. Never get caught with your defenses down. There is
no room for vulnerability. Weapons are vital to survival.

The build-up of nuclear warheads is simply a large
scale example of the fall, of Adam hiding in the bushes, of
one person passing on fear and violence to another.

Unfortunately, when those who are entrusted with
tending the earth are desperately in need of tending

themselves, they can only spread their "boshness." Unable to be reverent toward the land and the great bodies of water, they pollute them with chemical spills and poisoned runoff. No longer co-nurturers with the soil and seas, they contaminate the food supply and kill the fish as they seek to meet their own isolated needs. Like the by-products of their progress, they are too tainted to be faithful to the vision of mutuality.

The air, symbol of God's life-giving breath, wedded to the divine at the dawn of creation, is now foul with acid rain and smog. Our environment continues to suffer from the relentless urge to claim greater control over nature, the desire to take a bigger bite out of the magical apple that will make us like gods.

These are heartbreaking reminders of the ongoing failure of mutuality. They are some of the signposts of a lost vision.

If our globe bears the signs of the fall, so does our church. We need only look at her women and her men, separated into women's guilds and men's clubs, convents and rectories, chancery offices and motherhouses, "laity" and "religious." Too often God's daughters and sons work in separate directions, at separate meetings, developing separate goals and dreaming separate dreams. Over time we have become accustomed to these divisions and take them for granted. We forget that separations based on sexual differences stand in stark contrast to the God who called us into the partnership of male and female.

This is not to say that women cannot gather with other women, or that men cannot gather with other men for mutual support and sharing. All the same, we perpetuate the fall each time we make separateness the rule, or settle into complacency when one sex or the other is conspicuously excluded from our gatherings.

We perpetuate the fall each time we think we can carry the church into the future without each other, without that fundamental partnership on which the creative vision rests.

We perpetuate the fall each time we think we can strengthen the church by holding on more tightly to power. This feeble attempt to maintain control, this secret desire to function with the nature of a god, drives us away from community and ultimately away from God.

We perpetuate the fall each time we address one another as "sister" or "father" or "brother" or use the term "religious" in an exclusive way, forgetting that these titles belong not just to a special group in the church, but to all of God's children who yearn for partnership.

We perpetuate the fall each time we speak against racism, militarism, classism and sexism, and naively expect that true unity can be promoted among different races, cultures and political ideologies, from within a church led by an all male, all celibate, hierarchically arranged body.

We perpetuate the fall each time male, celibate church leaders use women and lay persons as consultants, and then make major decisions and give final approval to church documents in closed session.

We perpetuate the fall each time we think we can address the threat of nuclear holocaust, provide moral guidance for people, interpret the scriptures, teach theology, or find solutions for suffering people, without doing all of this as women and men in partnership with each other.

We perpetuate the fall each time we issue ultimatums from behind our desks and refuse face to face dialogue with the very people whose lives will be affected by our decisions.

We perpetuate the fall each time we forget that the women who pour out their blood and consecrate life on delivery room tables have enough of God's creative nature to consecrate bread and bless wine at the altars of our churches.

Our faithfulness to partnership needs to go beyond lip service and polite gestures. Male-female partnership is a biblical call deep within our natures. It is placed there by a God who preferred relating to isolation, revealing to hiding, a God who thought that women and men together was a much better idea than either of them alone.

Some theologians have suggested that the fundamental threat to humanity, the most basic "ism" of all is not racism, communism, classism, or militarism, but sexism. It is the one from which all other forms of division flow. When the two fundamental units of humanity, the male and the female persons, do not stand in mutuality, they have no experience on which to build mutuality among people of differing races, cultures, religions or political ideologies. The only spirituality that can heal our troubled globe is one that aims to restore the full partnership of the male-female vision.

Even though the author of Genesis 2 recognized that the signs of the fall were more evident than the signs of partnership, he chose not to let the vision die at the hands of a patriarchal society. The Old Testament writers were prophets of hope, not doom. They knew from life experience that the original state of male-female mutuality no longer existed. They saw that God's vision had been forgotten, but they believed that it would not be irrevocably lost. Their writings reveal their belief in the vision and their hope in its strength. In the end their message is simple:

> Yahweh fashioned partnership.
> Women and men lost it.
> Yahweh will restore it.

Tne Greatest of Songs: Partnership Restored

The Song of Songs represents a glimpse of this restoration. It is a hymn of faith in the future of partnership. Regarded by many scholars as a *midrash* (a kind of Hebrew homily) on Genesis 2, the Song of Songs must be read alongside the tragic story of Adam and Eve.

In Genesis 2 and 3, mutuality is destroyed. The man and the woman become ashamed of their nakedness. They hide from each other and from God. They do not speak to one another. They are separated by roles, each with a distinct set of life tasks. They go their way in toil. The woman is subordinate to the man and the garden is no longer their home. Each of these descriptions, it must be remembered, are results of the fall, rather than divinely intended conditions. Role dependence, female subordination, the absence of shared dialogue or erotic delight: these are all the sad effects of the failure of God's creative intention.

But tragedy is never God's last word. The Hebrew poets believed that mutuality would one day be restored. They needed a story, an image to pass on their hope. So they take us to another garden.

In the Song of Songs, the woman and the man are back in the garden. The forbidden tree of knowledge has given way to flowering pomegranate trees, blossoming vineyards, and inviting palms:

> "I will climb the palm tree,
> I will seize its clusters of dates"
>
> (Sg 7:8).

The garden is utterly safe and has no limit of delights. It harbors no hidden corners or forbidden places. The lilies are in bloom and the animals are playful.

If the setting of the garden is restored, the relationship between the woman and the man is even more so. Back in the garden, where they had experienced the initial joy of companionship, they now share a new mutuality born of grown up love. Again, they are naked and unashamed. They celebrate the beauty of their bodies, fully experiencing their flesh with all of its dignity and passion.

Role dependence is gone. We do not know if they are married, for they are not referred to as husband or wife, mother or father. There is no attempt to make their erotic union "proper." They are simply there for each other in primordial mutuality, a mutuality regarded as redemptive.

Stereotypes are also gone. The woman is bold, strong and initiating. The man is tender, gentle and verbally expressive. While patriarchal marriage is absent in the poetry, some important qualities of human love and relationality are clearly emphasized. Tenderness, fidelity and intimacy stand in the foreground of the interaction. There is a constant interplay of dialogue between the two. They communicate their feelings and name their experience for one another. They are refreshingly comfortable with their bodies. There is no ridicule, no manipulation. They are a woman and a man redeemed, a woman and a man naked and without shame, a woman and a man witnessing to the vision of mutuality.

The erotic imagery of the Song of Songs has often been an embarrassment to Christians. An attitude of sexual denial is evident in the way the church has interpreted and used (or rather, not used) the Song of Songs. In the past, spiritual writers taught that the poetry was not talking about a relationship between a woman and a man, but rather about a spiritual (and therefore, not embodied) relationship between God and Israel, or between God and the individual soul. This allegorical interpretation is an over-spiritualization of the story. It is also an affront to the God who fashioned bodies and created erotic passion.

Contemporary scholars have urged us to let the love poetry in the Song of Songs function as the poet originally intended it: as a description of restored mutuality among women and men, women and men who have bodies, who experience sexual arousal, and who are capable of making responsible, faithful and loving choices with regard to relationships.

The Song of Songs expresses the hope that the oppression of the fall will someday come to an end and that God's vision will once again be restored. It offers a promise that women and men will again experience their nakedness without shame and will relate to one another without masks or the barriers of secret thoughts and expectations. The poetry waits for the day when women and men will stand, as they did at the dawn of creation, speaking their words face to face before the God who made them and who entrusted them with the care of the earth.

4
The Festive Table
Jesus and Partnership

The Dangerous Memory of Jesus

In one of his books Edward Schillebeeckx refers to
what he calls "the dangerous and subversive memory of
Jesus of Nazareth." Many Christians might be puzzled at
this way of describing the one whom they revere as savior. Perhaps this is because spiritual writers have so frequently portrayed the rabbi from Nazareth in rather in-
nocuous terms, seeing him as a moral teacher who
emphasized a "generic ethic" of caring for people and
serving God. In the classic lives of Christ, Jesus is often
pictured in gentle, pastel shades of kindness. He reaches
out to the poor and the outcast, heals the physically and
emotionally afflicted and works other miracles to demonstrate the coming of God's kingdom into the world. In
these same works, his passion and death are frequently
interpreted in terms of a vicarious suffering for our sins,
a painful death that came about because of humanity's
sinfulness and the mysterious ways of divine provi-
dence.

This may be an edifying portrait of divine love and
mercy, but little about it suggests that Jesus is particu-

larly dangerous or subversive. If anything, we are left wondering why the religious and civil authorities in the first century were so antagonistic toward such a gentle and compassionate man. There appears to be very little in this traditional image of Jesus to warrant such a hostile response from his contemporaries.

There are historical reasons for this theologically disconnected portrait of Jesus, reasons rooted in the way Christology has developed over the centuries. It is related to the perennial temptation to "dis-incarnate" the person of Jesus. If Jesus of Nazareth, the Jewish rabbi, is removed from the social and political conflicts of his age, his significance can easily become overspiritualized and abstract. His message is then reduced to a private ethic of imitation.

What is missing in this portrait is the prophetic demands the life and teaching of Jesus make, not only on individuals, but also on the social and religious structures of every age. Over the centuries there has been a tendency to tame this message by adapting it to the cultural values of the day. In some instances, the scriptures have even been used to justify ethical and social behavior that are in fact contrary to the vision of the gospel.

In the last 30 years there has been a strong movement to recover the meaning of Jesus. This search has challenged theology to go beyond some of the previous cultural assumptions regarding the meaning of salvation. It has raised the age-old questions in a new context: What is at the heart of Jesus' teaching? To whom is it addressed? What are its implications for human life? Why did his message and life have such a threatening impact on the religious and political leaders of his time? Why was Jesus put to death?

In order to answer these questions biblical scholars and theologians have returned to the social and political setting of first-century Palestine with a fresh perspective and new historical tools. They have attempted to rediscover the fears and hopes, the suffering and dreams of the people with whom Jesus shared life and history. The result has been a significant shift in Christology away from a private, individualized view of salvation toward a more communal and contextual understanding. Liberation theology, for example, views Jesus not only as someone who "went about doing good" (cf. Acts 10:38) on behalf of individual people, but as someone whose message and deeds confronted the unjust social, religious and political structures of his day.

This shift in Christology from a private to a systemic perspective provides us with a fresh viewpoint on the concerns Jesus brought to his ministry. It also helps us to understand the violent reaction his teaching evoked in the political and religious leaders of the time. What was there about Jesus and his teaching that called forth such fear? At what point did the religious leaders begin to view him as more than an eccentric rabbi who had a rather casual approach to cultic purity and the Torah? What is the deeper meaning and import of Jesus' teaching? What is it that makes him "dangerous and subversive"?

To answer these questions, we must explore some of the social structures and religious assumptions that characterized Jewish life in the first century. We must understand more clearly the dehumanizing presence of the Romans and the fears of the Jewish religious leaders. Only when we begin to understand that Jesus was calling for an entirely new basis for human relationships does the deeper challenge of the gospel begin to emerge.

In this chapter we will examine some of these important background factors present in first-century Palestine. We will then explore the ways in which Jesus challenged these fundamental assumptions by living and preaching an "alternative vision," a radical new way of life, which called for partnership as the model of all human relationships.

THE SOCIAL AND RELIGIOUS BACKGROUND OF FIRST-CENTURY PALESTINE

Ethnic Exclusivity

Despite the universalist vision of Deutero-Isaiah,

Jewish society did not, in general, value a spirit of inclusivity toward other peoples. Centuries of wars, deportation and persecution had created a defensive mentality.

Like most other ethnic groups, the Jews understood their primary loyalty to be toward their own kin. Although Palestine, by reason of its geography and trade routes, was a meeting place of nations, it was not a melting pot of peoples. The Roman military presence created a simmering hatred toward the occupying powers and in turn stirred up suspicion and fear among citizens of Palestine. Even within the Semitic people there was division and misunderstanding. The Jews and the Samaritans, who shared a common religious and ethnic heritage, viewed one another with disdain and a spirit of mutual hostility that made any dialogue between them all but impossible.

This stance of social exclusivity is revealed in the daily use of language. In normal discourse, the members of other nations were often not even granted the status of personhood. The most common Jewish term for Gentiles was "dogs," a label that became part of everyday use. In Mark's gospel there is an account of a Syro-Phoenician woman who comes to Jesus and begs him to cast out an unclean spirit from her daughter. Jesus, possibly quoting a popular Jewish aphorism, responds that "the children [the Jews] should be fed first, because it is not fair to take the children's food and throw it to the dogs" (Mk 7:27). The remarkable thing about this incident is that the woman, in her persistent faith, successfully invites Jesus himself toward a more inclusive ministry.

The Marginated and the Forgotten

Even within the Jewish community there was an inherent social and religious caste system. The upper classes did not associate comfortably with the lower classes; the more affluent, urban Jews of Judea looked down upon the *am ha-aretz*—the "people of the land" who lived in Galilee and other parts of Palestine.

Life in first-century Palestine was for the most part

harsh and brutal. Only those with money and power could enjoy the few comforts of the day. What our contemporary culture takes for granted as essential to our daily welfare would have been considered a life of privilege at that time. The ordinary citizen had to struggle for the basics of life—food, shelter, clothing. There was a small middle class consisting of merchants, those who lived by a trade or a craft, and those who worked the land.

The stark reality is that the majority of people lived in poverty and deprivation. There were few medical resources to combat disease and no insurance or social programs that could reach out to alleviate suffering. Life-expectancy was short; the emotionally, mentally and physically handicapped were everywhere. This created a class of people who, no matter what their ethnic or religious background, were in reality outsiders, rejected by the rest of society, and left to die or cope for themselves as best they could. In addition to the poor, the sick and the disabled, this group also included tax collectors and prostitutes, both of whom were characterized as "sinners." This appelation was as much a social category as it was an ethical label. The deprivation of their lives and the oppressive structures of society locked them in to the very behaviors for which they were condemned.

The Patriarchal Structure of Family Life

The concrete historical data regarding the role of women in Roman and Jewish society prior to and at the beginning of the Christian era is sketchy at best. We simply do not have much evidence from daily life. We can only presume certain attitudes and practices from the available literature and the scant evidence we do have.

One thing is clear. The Jewish writings and the religious structures they reflect give us a picture that is obviously androcentric and patriarchal. This probably reflects the situation in daily life, even though scholars generally agree that the language of the Torah and other prescriptions of the Jewish Law are more restrictive than the actual social practice. In rabbinic Judaism, for instance, women are usually categorized with children and slaves. On the other hand, we have several biblical stories that portray a more initiating role for women. Women such as Hannah, Ruth and Esther reflect roles of strong leadership and wisdom. Most likely these women are prophetic exceptions to the rule.

In point of fact, the basis of personal relationships in Jewish social life was the patriarchal ordering of family life. This is reflected in the Hebrew laws and customs that reveal a clear pattern of male domination. Women were not permitted, for the most part, to take a public role, but were confined to childbearing, child rearing and domestic life. Similarly, women could not own property in their own name, nor could they initiate a divorce.

The blood line was likewise traced through the male line of ancestry. This is significant because the bond of blood relationship held a very high social priority in Jewish life.

The Hierarchical Structure of Jewish Religion

The primacy of the male in family life was paralled by the hierarchical structure of Jewish religious life. The most respected form of religious activity at this time in the history of Israel was the office of priesthood. It was the privilege of this group to offer ritual sacrifice in the Jerusalem temple on behalf of the rest of Israel. This cultic activity was not only relegated to males, but to a specific group of males who could trace their origins (whether through blood or political connection) to the tribe of Levi.

The religious life of Judaism was not limited to the temple or to the priestly caste. Even in the local synagogue, however, its leadership reflected an exclusively male prerogative and a hierarchical structure. The rabbinic tradition, which had arisen in the second century B.C.E., found its primary expression at the time of Jesus in the Pharisaical movement. For historical and theological reasons in the early Christian communities, the Pharisees received a negative image in the New Testament writings. In actuality they were a progressive, lay-based movement that expanded the religious experience and vision of Judaism beyond the temple to the synagogue. The focus of synagogue worship was the Torah—the reverent study and meticulous keeping of the Law of God. Women could attend the synagogue (sitting separately from the men), but only men could read and comment on the Law and the Prophets. Only men could officially study the Law and learn the nuances of interpretation as they were embodied in the various official schools. Like cultic worship in the Jerusalem temple, the study of God's word and its proclamation in the synagogue was considered to be the prerogative of educated Jewish males.

Temple and Torah: Metaphors of Jewish Religion

Obviously, there were other religious and political groups in Israel besides the Priests and Pharisees. Among these other movements were the Zealots, who were convinced that the temple priesthood was corrupt, and who advocated a holy war against the Roman oppressors. With the discovery of the Qumran scrolls in this century we've also come to know more about the Essenes, a pious, monastic-like movement of men who withdrew into the desert to await the final intervention of God into human history.

Even these more radical groups in Jewish society shared a male and hierarchical set of assumptions. All of the various reform groups took for granted, whether positively or negatively, that the central experience of Jewish faith revolved around cultic worship and adherence to the Law of God.

Thus, the Judaism into which Jesus was born focused on two religious images or symbols: Temple and Torah.

The Ordinary Jew and Religious Faith

There is a sad irony in the fact that Temple and Torah were the primary metaphors of religious practice in first-century Judaism. In reality these two institutions were detached from the everyday religious experience of ordinary Jewish people. The essential worship of the temple belonged to an elite group of priests. Even the ordinary adult male in the rest of society was reduced to a peripheral or observing role in its ritual cult. The women and the children were entirely excluded from any direct participation in temple worship.

As for the Torah, this also had become the domain of a religious elite. The Pharisees and the Scribes, in their enthusiasm for the Law, had developed a complicated system of interpretation and legal strictures that automatically excluded the majority of Jewish people. Some were ritually unclean or legally unfit by circumstances of their lives: women, lepers, the blind, physically disabled or handicapped, the mentally ill, the possessed, tax collectors, prostitutes and other "sinners." In short, the majority of Jewish people were excluded from or considered to be unworthy of both Temple and Torah.

THE RESPONSE OF JESUS

How did Jesus respond to the crises of his age? What was his stance before the Roman military presence and the exclusiveness of Jewish religion? How did he understand his ministry?

Jesus of Nazareth was a Jew. We cannot ignore this fundamental fact in trying to understand his meaning for our lives. He inherited a religious movement with a rich tradition and a history that spanned many centuries. From his youth Jesus prayed the psalms and read the sacred writings of his ancestors. He carried their memories in his blood and their dreams in his heart. From the point of view of great civilizations and political powers, his life seems peripheral and lost in obscurity.

He was born in what was considered a backward region of the civilized world. He was raised not in the urban, more cultured centers of Judea and Jerusalem, but in the rural, hill country of Galilee.

The first-century Jewish historian, Josephus, records a Zealot uprising in Galilee during the time that Jesus would have been a young boy. The Romans, we are told, responded to this political protest with ruthless violence. The memory of this incident would have been a vivid part of Jesus' youth. In the times in which he grew up, Jesus had to wrestle with the same question every Jew confronted: How can we be God's holy and priestly people under a foreign, godless regime?

These are not rhetorical questions. They are life and death issues of the heart. They are questions that every Jewish man and woman had to resolve for themselves. How did Jesus answer them? What made his response distinctive, even unique? What was the prophetic stance that made his ministry "dangerous and subversive"?

Commitment to a Relational Life

If we look beyond the individual encounters Jesus has with people in the gospel pericopes and reflect instead on their collective significance, a clear pattern begins to emerge like an undertow of truth or a mosaic of meaning with profound implications.

In his public ministry Jesus appears to resemble many of the other rabbis of his time: He is a wandering prophet and teacher, a *hasid* whose pattern of teaching is rooted in the wisdom tradition and grounded in compassion. But there is something essentially different about Jesus, something that does not fit the manner and approach of his contemporaries among the Scribes and Pharisees. Scholars continue to debate whether or not Jesus might have been a disciple in a rabbinical school or had some connection with the Essene community perhaps through John the Baptist. The gospels themselves give us no information regarding such a background. If anything, the questions of the crowds seem to presuppose that Jesus had no formal rabbinical training. Like other rabbis Jesus did have disciples, but here again the parallels are limited. In short, although Jesus came from the rabbinic tradition of Israel, the differences in his approach and his way of living are far greater than the things he has in common with his contemporaries.

What is different about Jesus? What sets him apart from the other rabbis of his time? It is his commitment to live a *relational* life. From the very beginning, Jesus chose not to "go it alone." This does not mean that he avoided solitude or that he did not encounter times of profound loneliness in his life. Jesus faced the loneliness of carrying his life and his commitments. He knew that his ministry would place him at odds with the religious and political institutions of his day. It is understandable that he frequently sought out times of solitude and prayer. But he never chose a pathway of isolation. He was not a "spiritual lone ranger," who appeared mysteriously on the horizon of human history, saved humankind from its brokenness and sin, and then disappeared into a celestial sunset. Before Jesus healed a leper or cast out a demon, before he told a parable or multiplied loaves, he began to form a community of women and men around him. It's a simple fact that we dare not take for granted: The one whom Christianity claims as Lord and brother chose not to be a "solo savior," but rather entered deeply into the mystery of relationships.

Like the other rabbis, Jesus had followers, but his relationship with his disciples was unlike any other rabbi in history. Jesus moved beyond the usual master/disciple model available in Palestinian Judaism, or for that matter in any other religious setting of the time. In the accounts the evangelists provide we can discern a subtle but clear development in the relationship between Jesus and his followers. This development finds its culmination in Jesus' words given to us in John's gospel: "I no longer call you servants, because servants do not know what their master is about. No, I call you friends, because I have made known to you everything that I have learned from the Father" (cf. Jn 15:15).

Jesus and the Torah

Jesus did not limit himself to passing on an interpretation of the Torah, as was the case with the other rabbis. He moved beyond law to relationship, beyond hermeneutics to personal commitment. He didn't ask his followers to risk their lives on a particular exegesis of the Law, but he did ask them to stake their lives and their integrity on following him. Jesus asked for total commitment to him as a person, even as he promised total dedication of his life for the sake of his followers and on behalf of all humanity.

Jesus' perspective went beyond the various schools of legal interpretation to transform the meaning of God's relationship with human persons. When the religious leaders of Israel voiced their dismay at his seeming neglect of traditional Jewish religion, Jesus only pushed them further. "I have not come to destroy the Law," he told them, "but to bring it to fulfillment" (cf. Mt 5:17).

A New Relationship With God

What does Jesus mean by bringing the Law to fulfillment? On the one hand, it appears that he wanted to return the Torah to its roots in the covenant between Israel and Yahweh; to re-ground it in its primordial setting of relationality and loving partnership. On the other hand, Jesus saw himself as completing or realizing the earlier covenant through his intimate relationship with the Abba-God of his life. Jesus experienced himself as "the beloved one of God," Israel's promise brought to fulfillment. He, in turn, invited others to experience and affirm that same covenantal relationship of love in their lives.

A New Basis of Relationships Among People

In reflecting on Jesus' experience of God and the impact of this in his relationship with humanity, we have touched upon one of the key factors that makes him "dangerous and subversive." Because Jesus claims a different relationship with God, he also proclaims a new relationship among human beings. If, through the experience and consciousness of Jesus of Nazareth, everyone can gain access to becoming "the beloved of God," then human and religious structures must take on a radical new form. It is no longer possible to accept hierarchical and patriarchal patterns as divinely pre-ordained structures in human life. If God has entered into partnership with humanity, human persons must in turn enter into partnership with one another.

Several scenes in the gospels embody Jesus' radically new approach to human relationships. Perhaps the most striking of these is found in Mark 3:31–35. This pericope also has parallels in Luke 11:15–22 and Matthew 12:24–32, but Mark's version is clearly the earlier and more straightforward account. It is significant that this passage occurs as part of a sequence of events in which the Jewish religious leaders, Jesus' disciples, and even his own family are having difficulty accepting his message and his ministerial behavior.

Jesus is preaching in a house crowded with people who have come to hear him. "His mother and his brothers now arrived and, standing outside, they sent in a message asking for him" (Mk 3:31). The crowd informs Jesus that his family are asking for him. In the Jewish value system, blood relationship is the closest and most demanding of all ethical bonds. There would have been an assumption among those assembled that Jesus would immediately respond to his family's desire to see him. Instead, Jesus asks a question: "Who are my mother and my brothers?" (3:33). And then, Mark adds these highly symbolic words: "And looking around at *those sitting in a circle about him* he said, "Here are my mother and my brothers. Anyone who does the will of God, that person is my brother and sister and mother'" (3:35, italics ours).

This is more than a convivial story of inclusiveness or personal hospitality. Jesus is directly confronting the long-standing structure of the patriarchal family, as well as the accepted Jewish vision of gender inequality and ethnic exclusivity. He replaces these traditional structures of human relationships with a far more radical criterion, namely, hearing the word of God and keeping it. The circle of human community is, like divine love itself, an open and inclusive embrace of all. The implications of this stance are truly revolutionary. Jesus is calling upon people to be compassionate and loving not only within their accepted social and religious parameters, but to transcend all humanly contrived boundaries in order to establish "a discipleship of equals."

A New Understanding of Leadership

In a world that assumed political and religious power as the capacity to coerce others into servility, Jesus offers an alternate way of human leadership. He rejects any form of authority that exploits or demeans women and men by turning them into "subjects." Instead he calls his followers to become "servant-leaders" who reject the usual displays of position and privilege.

This aspect of Jesus' teaching was apparently one of the most difficult for his followers to understand or accept. It contradicted everything their culture had taught them about the hierarchical ordering of society and religious institutions. It stood in direct opposition to their expectations of the messiah and his role in the political restoration of Israel.

In a scene all three synoptics record (Mk 10:42–45; Mt 20:25–28; Lk 22:25–27), Jesus confronts the disciples' misunderstanding and shares his radical vision of leadership. In each case the disciples have been arguing about who will hold the places of honor in the coming kingdom. The response of Jesus varies slightly in each of the evangelists, but the underlying message is the same: Leadership is loving service, not the quest for dominating power. Over the centuries the argument that broke out among the original disciples has erupted again and again with predictable regularity. The response to this argument has never changed: "Among the pagans it is the kings who lord it over them, and those who have authority over them are given the title Benefactor. This must not happen with you . . ." (Lk 22:25–26).

Jesus and the Call to Partnership

We return to our earlier question. In what sense is Jesus "dangerous and subversive"? What is it about his memory that subverts our easy assumptions about the gospel?

Is it related to his values and his way of ministering to others? Is Jesus dangerous because he broke the barriers of Jewish cultic law and reached out to the ritually unclean? Is he subversive because he went beyond the strictures of the rabbinic code and welcomed those who could not keep the Torah in the legalistic manner of the Pharisees?

The answer to each of these questions is yes. But this acknowledgement lacks something. It does not say enough. It does not capture the depth with which Jesus challenges the usual standards of religious conformity. Jesus is dangerous not just because he related to people beyond the boundaries of religious propriety or beneath him on the social ladder. Jesus is subversive because he proclaims and lives an entirely new basis for human relationships. Jesus teaches that women and men are called into a community of loving, equal discipleship.

In the end, it is not the Temple or the Torah that Jesus proclaims as holy. It is the *people* who are holy—all of the people, but especially those who are not considered acceptable in the patriarchal and hierarchical structures of the time: the poor, the sinners, the outcast, tax collectors, foreigners, women, children and slaves.

The metaphor Jesus uses to describe the reign of God is not related to cultic worship or the legal prescriptions of the law. It conjures up the image of a banquet the creator has prepared for all God's daughters and sons. Jesus' image for the reign of God is the *festive table* to which all people are invited and welcomed as partners. This festive table breaks down the usual barriers and divisions between people. There are no separate tables in the kingdom. It is no longer political or religious status that counts. It is no longer gender or economic class or racial background that is the determining factor. Only one thing matters—the willingness to see the world and its people with new eyes and an open heart.

5
Neither Male nor Female
Partnership in the Early Church

A Turning Point in History

In the autumn of 1974, as the synod on evangelization came to a close, Pope Paul VI gave each of the participating bishops a copy of the Acts of the Apostles. At the time this gift was intended as a simple gesture of hospitality, a reminder that the Acts of the Apostles is the premier model of Christian evangelization. But as the renewal initiated by Vatican II continues to unfold, Paul VI's gift takes on a deeper significance. We can think of it as a prophetic symbol that points beyond itself toward the deeper meaning of our age and the mission of the gospel in today's world.

The Acts of the Apostles is, in many ways, the biblical book of our times. It describes both the energy and the birthpangs that accompany a major time of transition. It resonates with the promise and presence of the Spirit, even as it reveals the volatility and frailty of human leadership.

In his book *Concern for the Church* Karl Rahner speaks of what he calls the "theological significance of the Second Vatican Council." In the history of Christianity, Rahner claims, there have been two major turning points or "axial periods." The first took place during the last half of the first century, in the decades following Jesus' death and resurrection. It involved the transition of Christianity from a Jewish sect into a "religion of the nations." The second great turning point is taking place in our time, in the wake of the Second Vatican Council, as the Catholic Church begins to shift from a Eurocentric focus toward the possibility of becoming, for the first time in history, truly a "world church."

THE ACTS OF THE APOSTLES AND THE CONTEMPORARY CHURCH

In this chapter we will explore the vision of partnership in the early church. Our starting point is the remarkable parallel between the story of Acts and the challenges that confront the contemporary church. The author of Luke/Acts probably wrote in the late 80s or early 90s of the first century. We are living in the late 80s and early 90s of the 20th century. As we move toward the third millenium of Christianity, we look back to our roots. We remember the energy with which the Good News burst into human history. What can we learn from the early communities of faith about trusting the Spirit? What can they teach us about partnership and living the gospel?

A New Age

The Christian scriptures remind us in various ways, both from the teaching of Jesus and the concerns of the early communities, that there is a fundamental continuity between the Hebrew vision of God and the Christian encounter with the risen Christ. Beyond continuity, however, there is another theme in the New Testament writings that we dare not ignore if we are to understand what it means to be "followers of the Way." This is the focus on the Jesus event as something that brings the brings the past to fulfillment and initiates something radically new.

Acts opens with the account of Pentecost as a new creation. The Spirit comes upon the community as a driving wind and as tongues of fire, recalling the primordial vision of Genesis. It invites us to touch again the initial act of cosmic creativity when the *ruach Elohim*—the wind or Spirit of God—moves out over the dark abyss to bring order and fiery energy into being. Pentecost is the birth of the church, the beginning of the new creation.

Transformed by the energy of the Spirit, the disciples begin to proclaim the risen Christ. In the book of Acts there are several discourses or sermons. These are not intended to be eyewitness accounts or verbatim reports, but they certainly contain the essential core of the *kerygma*—the original announcement of the Good News. It is striking, therefore, that when Peter addresses the crowds for the first time after Pentecost, his first words are in regard to the "new age" that has been inaugurated through the resurrection of Jesus and the outpouring of his Spirit on all humankind. In order to substantiate his claim of newness, Peter recalls the vision of the prophet Joel. Preaching in the post-exilic time of discouragement and broken dreams, Joel spoke of a new age when the Spirit would be poured out on everyone, not just on certain elite groups within Israel:

> "It shall come to pass in the last days,
>   says God,
> that I will pour out a portion of my spirit
>   on all humankind:
> Your sons and daughters shall prophesy,
> your young men shall see visions and
> your old men shall dream dreams.
> Yes, even on my servants and hand-
>   maids
> I will pour out a portion of my spirit in
>   those days..."
>   (Acts 2:17-18, *NAB*; cf. Joel 3:1-5).

When Pope John XXIII announced the Second Vatican Council, he referred to it as "a new Pentecost," a fresh beginning for the church. Only a few years later, as the council was coming to a close, the bishops of Vatican II echoed this same theme. "Ours is a new age of history," they declared in *Gaudium et Spes,* the Pastoral Constitution on the Role of the Church in the Modern World. More recently, the bishops of the United States reaffirmed the distinct challenge of our age in their pastoral letter on peace. They spoke of "a new moment" in human history, a moment laden with awesome possibilities; a moment of decision and responsibility; a moment when we will either choose the pathway of self-destruction through nuclear warfare, or the long, demanding road that leads toward peace; a moment when the energies of the earth and the dreams of humankind can be channeled toward a new community on this planet.

The Spirit Poured Out on All Humankind

The Acts of the Apostles is not only the story of the Spirit of God bursting anew into human life; it is also the story of the people who experienced the Spirit and proclaimed its presence and meaning to others. The remarkable truth about Joel's vision and its consequent fulfillment in Acts is that the coming of the Spirit is not limited to a patriarchal or hierarchical elite. It comes to dwell equally in the young and old, with women and with men, among the servants as well as free persons. In a religious culture whose assumptions and structures were strongly androcentric, this would have been startling news indeed. And yet, this is clearly what Acts proclaims as the essential reality of the new age. The good news of Jesus is that he has conquered death, division and alienation. He has become, in the words of Paul, "a life-giving Spirit" for all people.

The Spirit of Jesus is a boundary-breaking energy that disrupts the former configurations of power and influence. Where there had been Jacob's ladder there is now to be "Sarah's circle"; where there had been a hierachical ordering of cult and law, there is now to be a community of disciples and a discipleship of equals. Partnership is to replace patriarchy.

"God does not ration the Spirit," Jesus tells us in John's gospel (Jn 3:34). This abundance of the Spirit manifested itself in the early church and it is revealing itself again in our time. We read the story of Acts today with new insight and hope. Throughout the world we are reliving, at a deeper and more intense level of human life, the story of the primitive Christian communities.

We can learn a great deal from the early communities of faith about the vision of partnership and the resourcefulness needed to pursue that vision. When the demands of ministry became greater than the number of persons who were available to meet them (cf. Acts 6:1-6), the early community did not lose heart. Trusting in the abundant resources of the Spirit, they came together in discernment and established new forms of ministry to meet the needs of the community. They welcomed those who felt called to engage in ministry—women and men alike.

The same phenomenon is taking place in the church today. In his book, *New Ministries*, William Burrows speaks of what he calls "wineskin-breaking ministries," which are emerging around the world at the grassroots of Christian life. The institutional leadership may have theological doubts about these new forms of partnership, but despite its hesitations, these ministries are continuing to respond to the needs of people throughout the world. They are manifestations today of the resourcefulness and abundant energy of the Spirit. They are contemporary proof, if we need proof, that today, as in the early church, "God does not ration the Spirit." Today, as in the first century, a divine energy is being unleashed both within and beyond the structures of the church.

Conflict and Creative Tension

We can make a third comparison between the Acts of the Apostles and the contemporary church. It has to do with the conflict and confusion that accompany any time of upheaval and radical transformation. Ordinarily, conflict is not a dimension of our lives with which we are especially comfortable, whether it is in our own personal relationships or in the social institutions in which we share. Perhaps this is because we find confrontation and division, no matter when or where it occurs, to be so painful and disillusioning.

For some reason, many people envision the early church as a serene community of faith in which unanimity and doctrinal accord were obvious qualities of life. This tendency to overidealize the first followers of Jesus comes, in the first place, from the author of Luke/Acts, who looks back on the Jerusalem community from the vantage point of almost 50 years and writes, with some nostalgia, about the early days of the Christian movement. His optimism may also flow from the normal tendency to suppress the painful and unpleasant memories of life. At any rate, he gives us the portrait of the early community as it is described in the early chapters of Acts (2:42-47; 4:32-35). It is an idyllic image of shared prayer, unity in mind and heart, meals taken together in joy, the equal distribution of goods, and a daily increase in the number of converts.

If this state of affairs did exist, it would have been for a rather brief period. It is also fair to say that this is the last time we see the church at peace in the New Testament. The rest of the story of Acts and the remainder of the Christian scriptures reflect a church in transition and upheaval, a church struggling to understand its mission and its identity; a community wrestling with the conditions of membership; a church attempting to take the life and teachings of Jesus and translate them into action; a community in which the Hebrew Christians and the Greek-speaking Christians are in ongoing tension; a community with factions and polarizations; a church in which Paul confronts Peter, and Antioch wrestles theologically with Jerusalem. In the midst of it all, women and men are learning together how to proclaim the good news of Christ as partners in the Spirit. It is, in short, a church in creative upheaval.

It should not be difficult for us to recognize this church. Its pain and its promise are strikingly similar to our own. We need only listen to the sounds of our growth: the rush of the Spirit in a fresh act of creation; the fire of new energy; women and men seeing visions and dreaming dreams. It is a new age of grace, the proclamation of a way of life that breaks down the centuries-old barriers of race, religion, social class and gender. And yes, there is also the chaos and pain that accompanies such a breakthough: divisions and factions, argument and confrontation, the confusion of uncertainty; the burden of choosing and then carrying one's decisions. All of these are the sights and sounds of dying and rising, the sure price of being born anew. This is the deeper memory of the Acts of the Apostles. It is also the present intensity of a church reclaiming the power of partnership.

The Acts of the Apostles is to the Christian scriptures what Genesis is to the sacred writings of the Hebrews. It introduces the vision. It gives us a glimpse of the divine intention and of our human possibilities. It tells us of ancient longings brought to fulfillment, of a boundary-breaking Spirit and of wineskin bursting ministries. It also gives us, like the first notes of a symphony, the thematic pattern of conflict and upheaval that accompanies all growth.

PATTERNS OF PARTNERSHIP IN THE EARLY CHURCH

With the vision of Acts as a thematic background, we turn now to the specific forms partnership took in the early church. How seriously did the first communities take the life and teaching of Jesus? To what extent did they attempt to embody his vision and to live out his approach to leadership and community? What role did women play in the proclamation of the gospel and in the forming of faith communities?

Women as Apostles

Until recently, our presumptions about the scriptures have been strongly influenced by an androcentric point of view. As a result, we have virtually ignored one of the most obvious lessons of the post-resurrection accounts, namely that the evangelists portray Mary of Magdala and the other faithful women as models of Easter faith and discipleship.

Even though women are not explicitly given the title "apostles" in the four gospels, they do fulfill the conditions for apostleship in a premier way. The Pauline writings give two criteria for being an apostle: 1) to have seen the risen Lord, and 2) to be commissioned by him to preach the good news. Later, the Lucan writings add another criterion: 3) to have accompanied Jesus during his earthly life. It is clear in all four gospels that the faithful women, Mary of Magdala, Mary the mother of James, and Salome, fulfill all three of these conditions. They are the first to encounter the empty tomb and to see the risen Lord. They are in turn "sent" by him to the rest of the community with the news of his resurrection: "Go and tell my brothers [and sisters] that they must leave for Galilee: they will see me there" (Mt 28:10).

Contemporary scholarship has established that the word "apostle" is strictly speaking a post-resurrection term. It is not limited to "the Twelve" or to men. In the Pauline letters the term "apostle" is given to women and to men, indeed to anyone who carries out the work of proclaiming the good news of the risen Christ. Thus it was taken for granted in the early communities that Jesus intended his mission and ministry to be carried out in a collaborative effort involving both women and men in partnership.

Charismatic Prophets: Early Forms of Partnership

Recent scripture studies have begun to focus on the social setting of the New Testament as a way of gaining greater insight into the background and context of the early Christian writings. Using the most recent evidence gathered from archeological findings and other forms of research, scholars have delved into the layers of culture that lie beneath the written versions of our gospels. They have helped us to understand what were likely the earliest experiences of the "Jesus movement" in Palestine in the years immediately following the resurrection. Relying on the collection of *logia* or "sayings" of Jesus, which are found in the "Q" source (the earlier source from which both Luke and Matthew drew, in addition to their reliance on Mark), a fascinating picture of the first preachers of the good news begins to appear. When this information is combined with what we can glean from the early writings of Paul, we can begin to construct a clearer, though still sketchy picture of post-resurrection ministry.

Who were these early proclaimers of the gospel? The evidence suggests they were itinerant preachers compelled by the energy of the Spirit and filled with the desire to share the meaning and implications of the resurrection event. They included women as well as men who travelled from place to place as charismatic prophets. They imitated the Master in their spirit of simplicity and their availability to the outcasts of society. Their lifestyle was characterized by a renouncement of home, family and possessions. Their preaching focused on the victory of Jesus over death and his imminent return as the Lord of history.

In some instances these wandering charismatics may have worked alone. More often, however, they followed the mandate of Jesus to go forth "two by two" in shared ministry. In Paul's letters it is clear that many of these partnerships were women and men, who ministered in mutuality. The Pauline writings give us the names of some of these partners: Priscilla and Aquila, Junia and Andronicus, and others. These names are important clues to the style of the earliest Christian ministry. Many of them were preaching the good news and forming communities of faith long before Saul of Tarsus was converted to the Way and joined the Christian missionary movement. Even after his conversion it is clear that he looked to them with respect, even with a certain deference.

The Western tradition of Catholicism since the 12th century has been dominated by a male, celibate form of leadership. We easily forget that many of the earliest ministers were married couples. We know that some of the twelve themselves may have been married and were probably accompanied by their wives in ministry. In addition to the missionary couples who were married, there may have been brother-sister partnerships. There is even some historical evidence that women and men who were not married, but committed to celibacy, also functioned as missionary partners in the beginnings of the Christian movement.

Household Churches: The Context of Partnership

The church with which most of us are familiar is a highly organized institution, a network of authority and administration, a flow chart of specific offices, programs and bureaucracies. When we say "church" many of us picture chancery offices, marriage tribunals, diocesan newspapers, colleges, seminaries and mailing lists. We have an image of the classic parish with its church, school, convent (now often vacated or used for another purpose) and of course the rectory. We picture the parish offices furnished with word processors, copy machines, file cabinets and an answering machine.

When we think of the wider Catholic church, we imagine the 800 million people throughout the world who claim this tradition as their own—a world-wide potpourri of communities, who, whatever their ethnic or racial heritage, or however diverse their pastoral needs and devotional expressions, are linked by a shared history, a sacramental life and a common profession of faith.

This vast network of people and cultures is currently undergoing a major transformation in its self-understanding and mission. During this time of transition the primary energy of renewal is coming, not from the institutional leadership, but from the grassroots experience of people. It is no accident that the church is relying more and more on the need for strong family life (the "domestic church") and on the emergence of small, intentional communities of faith.

There is no better introduction to the early experience of partnership ministry than the contemporary phenomenon of small Christian groups. If we are to understand the life of the early communities of faith that emerged in the decades following the resurrection, we have to shift our perspective from large institutions of power to small communities of faith. The church emerged from people in relationship. It came into being in an upper room and thrived in similar settings throughout the Mediterrean world. From the evening of Jesus' last passover and the Pentecost event to the "peace of Constantine" the seed bed of Easter faith was the house-church.

What were these household communities? On what social and relational model were they based? How did they try to embody the teaching and example of Jesus regarding a discipleship of equals? What can we learn from them about partnership ministry?

The Greek word for household is *oikos* (from which we derive words such as economy and ecology). In Greco-Roman culture it referred to the social structure of the patriarchal family, which included the *paterfamilias* with his wife, children and live-in relatives, as well as the domestic servants and caretakers of the estate (depending on the economic status of the family). In many instances it also included elderly grandparents, uncles and aunts, in-laws and even business associates. Perhaps the closest image from our recent cultural past with which we can compare the Greco-Roman household is the extended family.

This sociological background gives us a better understanding of the phrase used frequently in the New Testament writings, describing the manner in which someone was converted to the Way "with all his house" (cf. Acts 16:15, 16:31-34; 1 Cor 1:16). The house-churches were a decisive influence in the spread of Christianity throughout the Hellenic world (cf. Fiorenza, p. 175 ff.). They provided the physical space in which to gather and the communal setting necessary for the faith to grow. They were an ideal environment to celebrate the tradition of prayer and table-fellowship that Jesus had initiated in his life and teaching. They also functioned as the "formation centers" for new missionaries. The theological impact of the house-churches is reflected in the language of the early missionary movement, which spoke of the believers as the "house of God" and the "new temple of the Spirit."

This brings us to a key factor in understanding the pastoral theology embodied in the house-churches. Since the patriarchal family was already the dominant cultural pattern, we might expect that the early Christians would simply adapt the gospel to this established social structure. In reality this was not the case. The followers of the Way did choose small, household communities in which to put the gospel into practice. They did not, however, accept the patriarchal family as the model for these communities. Instead they looked for a more collaborative form of community that went beyond the hierarchical structure of traditional Jewish religion and the patriarchal ordering of the Greco-Roman family.

They found the makings of this model in the voluntary associations which had, over time, begun to appear in the Roman empire. Some of these egalitarian groups were formed on the basis of a common trade or occupation. Others developed from the popular oriental religious cults that prominent military leaders were bringing back to the Roman empire. In Latin these egalitarian associations are called *collegia* (from which we derive our term collegial); in Greek the word is *thiasoi*. Usually these "free societies" were funded and sustained by a wealthy patron or patroness, but their membership was open to the freeborn or the freed, and in some instances even to women and slaves.

The similarities between the early Christian communities and the *collegia* are striking. But there are also significant differences. In effect, the followers of the Way transcended both the patriarchal family and the voluntary social organizations of the empire to create a new "alternative community." They welcomed the social rootedness of the Greco-Roman *oikia*, but divested it of its patriarchal ordering. They adopted the egalitarian model of the *collegia*, but transformed it into a community of faith and discipleship.

From the earliest stages of Christian community, women played a significant role of leadership along with men. In Hellenic society women had already begun to assume a greater role socially and economically than their counterparts in Judaism. Many commentators believe that the conflict between the Hebrews and the Hellenists in Acts 6 is more than just an issue of the unequal distribution of food. Hellenist women were used to taking part in various symposia and in festive dinners. The conflict could well have been between them and the more patriarchal male leaders in Jerusalem. Whatever the actual issues, it is clear that the villas, in which the house-churches gathered, were often owned by prominent and well-placed women who were attracted to Christianity. Even in Luke/Acts, which for theological reasons tends to neglect the active role of women, there are clear instances in which women are described as the founders and leaders of house-churches (e.g. Acts 12:12-17).

Circle of Charisms: The Style of Partnership

The house-churches provided a setting for Christians to take seriously the life and teachings of Jesus regarding human relationships. They were literally the seed bed ("seminary") in which the first communities of faith tried to translate Jesus' vision of inclusivity and equality into everyday life.

Most of our information about ministry in these communities comes from Paul's early letters to Corinth, Galatia, Rome and Thessalonica. These documents are rich sources of information and theological reflection. They reveal that the communities to which Paul ministered

were a complex, fluid network of local structures and relationships. Although we do not often pay much attention to it, there are in fact more than 80 personal names
mentioned in the letters of Paul. They include women
and men from all walks of life and ethnic backgrounds in
shared experiences of partnership. The various lists of
ministries (1 Cor 12:8-10, 28-30; Rom 12:6-8; Eph 4:11)
include preaching, teaching, prophesying, healing,
speaking with tongues, distinguishing spirits, interpret-
ing, table service, leadership and others.

What do these ministries have in common? First,
they are all referred to as *charismata* —gifts individuals
have for the purpose of building up the community. The
greatest of these *charismata*, and the one which binds
all the others together, is, of course, love.

Second, these ministries reveal a fundamental commitment to partnership: a vision of equality in the Spirit.
Many of the terms Paul uses are general descriptions of
ministerial partnership. Thus he speaks of the women
and men who are his *synergoi*—fellow workers or companions in ministry. Most likely this title did not refer to
any specific office in the church. Rather it was used to
designate anyone who helped build up the community
through ministry. Paul addresses several men as his
synergoi: Timothy, Mark, Demas, Luke, Aquila, Justus
and Epaphroditus. He also speaks of women in the same
way: Prisca, Synteche and Euodia, for example.

Another generic term Paul employs is *kopian* ("to
work hard"). From the context in which Paul uses this
word it appears that he is referring particularly to the
work of preaching and evangelization. In the letter to the
Romans, Paul names four women: Mary, Tryphaena,
Tryphosa and Persis as "hard workers in the Lord."
Thus, women as well as men functioned as prophets and
teachers (see also Acts 21:9). In some instances more
specific terms are given to women: Junia is called an
"apostle," Phoebe is referred to as a *diaconos*, a title that
ought not to be translated as "deaconess" since
diaconos is a form of ministry performed by both women

and men and carries a specific connotation of preaching and table presiding.

The pattern of ministry that emerges in the *ekklesia* of early Christianity has many background influences. Some of these formative tendencies come from the secular society of the day, for example, the Greco-Roman household or voluntary associations and clubs. Even the term *ekklesia* was likely derived from its civil usage, which referred to the assembly of free, male citizens of a city to hold elections. In Christianity it came to designate the assembly of the various house-churches in a city or local region, for example, the *ekklesia* of Corinth or Philippi. The followers of the Way also drew from the patterns of the Jewish synagogue and from the style of philosophical schools.

In the end, however, the Christian missionary movement is far more than its influences. Its vision and the embodiment of that vision cannot be identified with the religious hierarchy of Judaism or the social patriarchy of the Greco-Roman culture. It found useful models in the alternative communities that had sprung up in that age, but they could neither contain its message nor embody its sense of inclusivity. Christianity, in short, is a new and transforming energy of the Spirit. It is the festive table of the kingdom unfolding in house-churches. It is an attempt to enflesh the new basis of human relationships—the circle of disciples Jesus welcomed and affirmed as his own, the inclusive community of love for which he lived and died. It is the gospel proclaimed and lived, not from a pedestal of dominative power, but in a circle of charisms.

The Galatian Manifesto: The Vision of Partnership

How seriously did the early followers of Jesus take his teaching and example regarding equality and partnership between women and men? From the perspective of historical research, this question is difficult to answer. The earliest beginnings of Christianity are lost somewhere in the shadows of history. By the time Paul is writing letters to the communities of Asia Minor in the early 50s, almost two decades have passed since the resurrection of Jesus. We can only touch the earliest stages of the "Jesus movement" in Palestine and the Christian missionary efforts in the Diaspora through references, assumptions, and indirect evidence. This makes this evidence not less important but all the more valuable in understanding the foundations of Christian mission and ministry.

The earliest and most important center for the Christian missionary movement was the ancient city of Antioch, in what is now Syria. Ideally situated on the river Orontes, accessible from both land and sea, Antioch was the cosmopolitan crossroads of the Greco-Roman world, a center of trade, communication and culture. Here the early followers of the Way, probably Greek-speaking converts who experienced persecution in Jerusalem, came to form a community of faith. Their commitment to the gospel and to partnership ministry enabled them to become the most significant center of Christian evangelization in the first century.

This community of missionaries was already flourishing before Saul of Tarsus was converted. Its founders may well have been missionary couples. Most certainly its leaders included women and men, who, long before Acts was written, were forming "prophets and teachers" (Acts 13:1) and sending them forth to preach to the Gentiles. It was most likely here in Antioch that the theological vision of Christian mission was developed, and it is here that the followers of the Way become known as "Christians" for the first time (Acts 11:26).

Through Barnabas and others Paul became associated with this visionary group. He was probably influenced strongly by their theology and eventually became one of their leaders and certainly their most famous missionary. We cannot forget, however, that their work preceded Paul and continued to flourish independently of Paul.

Most commentators believe that when Paul writes to the Christians of Galatia he is quoting from the Antioch "missionary manifesto" to substantiate his claim of radical equality among the followers of Christ. This guiding vision is similar to what today we might call a "mission statement." It is found in Galatians 3:27-28:

> All baptized in Christ, you have all clothed yourselves in Christ, and there are no more distinctions between Jew and Greek, slave and free, male and female, but all of you are one in Christ Jesus.

There are several remarkable things about this mission statement. In the first place, it was articulated quite early in the missionary movement, probably in the early 40s. Although it appears as a brief and simple statement of purpose, it nevertheless represents a highly developed theology and pastoral vision. It also indicates how seriously the early Christians took the life and teaching of the Master. Obviously the implications of this vision are profound and sweeping. Living almost 20 centuries after it was first articulated, we can only admit with a certain sadness that the vision has never been fully realized.

A further dimension of the Galatians ministry statement deserves our attention. The manifesto looks to baptism as a transforming event that not only has spiritual and inward consequences, but social and political ones as well. The whole person is transformed by coming into relationship with the risen Christ: Gentiles are to be welcomed as brothers and sisters, slaves are to be freed, women are to be in equal partnership with men. It doesn't take a great deal of reflection on this mission statement to understand why Christians would eventually be persecuted. It is not only Jesus who is "dangerous and subversive," but also his followers. They too will threaten the long-accepted structures of oppression and exploitive power that exist at the center of almost every known culture.

Neither Jew nor Gentile

As we approach the beginning of the 21st century, our planet appears to grow smaller in its geographical horizons, even as it continues to expand in its social and cultural diversity. It is clearer to us now than ever before that the gospel cannot be limited to a single ethnic group.

But what we accept as a given today was not that obvious to those who first heard the good news of Jesus. If it was clear, the demands and implications of such a universalism were too much for most people to bear. As we have seen earlier, many of the disciples approached the Way as though it were simply an apocalyptic sect of Judaism. They believed that God had anointed Jesus as messiah, raised him from the dead and would send him soon in a second coming of glory to destroy the Roman oppressors and bring history to fulfillment.

Christianity could never have spread beyond Jerusalem and the Jewish community without the emerging conviction of its fundamental inclusiveness. When that conviction did emerge, its implications created painful divisions in almost every Christian community. Any illusions we have regarding the harmonious relationships among the early Christians ought to be realistically dispelled when we read of the confrontation and conflict this issue raised. Even after the council of Jerusalem decided to admit Gentiles without requiring them to be circumcized or keep all the Jewish dietary laws, the problem was far from settled. As late as the pastoral letters, close to the turn of the century, factions still demanded that Christianity return to a more exclusivist stance.

It is hardly necessary to remind ourselves that nationalism, ethnic discrimination and racism have continued to plague Christianity throughout the almost two millennia of its history.

Neither Slave Nor Free

The Roman empire, like most of the rest of the ancient world, was organized around a hierarchical ordering of society (cf. Osiek, p. 48 ff.). There were clear positions of superiority and subordination. At the top of the social order were two groups or *ordines* of aristocrats: (1) the senatorial *ordo,* whose members were eligible for the highest positions of honor; (2) the *ordo* of equestrians, a lesser aristocratic social stratum, whose members were often involved in regional administration of Rome's far-flung empire.

Below the ranks of the aristocrats were the freeborn lower classes, followed by the freedmen and freedwomen and finally the slaves. Urban slaves, who were involved in domestic, educational and, at times, administrative responsibilities, experienced their lot as much more tolerable than their counterparts in the mines and provinces. Some of them were even able to become rich and eventually purchase their freedom. No matter what the conditions, however, slavery was clearly a social reality of degradation and oppression. More than that, slavery was a vital and necessary component of the economic structure of the empire.

We must keep these realities in mind if we are to comprehend fully the threat Christianity would have posed to Greco-Roman culture. This is not just one more religious sect; this is a revolutionary vision of the human person and of societal structures. It is one thing to propose a new explanation of life. It is a far more serious matter when this new vision threatens to move beyond explanation to societal conversion. This is precisely what the Antioch missionary movement claimed on behalf of Christianity. Baptism was understood not just symbolically, but literally as a new creation. Oriental cults also initiated women and men, slave or free, as equals, but this was clearly understood to be a "private salvation" from the pain and inequity of the world. It had no social or political consequences. In the early stages of Christianity it had powerful and revolutionary consequences. Historical records tell us that early communities of Christians were expected to raise the necessary funds to purchase a slave's freedom in conjunction with his or her baptism.

The letter to Philemon gives us a glimpse of the social and economic implications of Christian baptism. Paul sends the newly baptized slave, Onesimus, back to Philemon with the expectation that he will no longer be a slave, but a beloved brother "both in the flesh and in the Lord" (Phlm 16). Clearly, Paul is referring both to the social and political reality of slavery and to his new-won freedom in Christ. What is all the more striking in this instance is that Paul possessed neither the legal ability to set Onesimus free himself, nor the authority to command Philemon to do so. He relies simply upon the full meaning of baptism, with the presumption of love that Philemon will accept Onesimus as a "beloved brother."

Neither Male Nor Female

Finally, the Galatians manifesto challenges the inherent patriarchal bias of the ancient world. What we today refer to as "sexism" was a social given in the Roman empire, a stance that had long been incorporated into the civil laws and the religious institutions of society. The teachings of the philosophers and the sacred writings of the major world religions had simply "blessed" what patriarchy had already been practicing. The Galatian missionary community, following the leadership of Jesus himself, confronted this inherent inequality. They named the social demon of exploitation and proclaimed a radically different alternative for Christian living.

The declaration of Galatians 3:28 cuts to the heart of patriarchal privilege (cf. Fiorenza, p. 205 ff.). It challenges the proclivity to maintain social stratification based on dominative or exploitive power. In effect, it denies all male religious prerogatives in the Christian community based on gender roles. The implications of the gospel are as clear in the relationships between women and men as they are in other social settings. Just as someone who was born into Judaism had to give up the privileged notion that they alone were the chosen people of God, and just as masters were asked to relinquish their power over slaves, so too husbands were expected to abandon the power they claimed over their wives and children.

The Antioch mission statement directly challenges those who use power and privilege to exploit people. But the manifesto also contains a positive dimension. It celebrates the energy of the Spirit that is released in authentic mutuality. It welcomes and affirms the partnership of women and men. The community at Antioch is not only declaring that dominative power is to be confronted, but that Easter power—the power of shared love and ministry—is to be affirmed as the true pathway to human transformation.

6
Partnership or Patriarchy?
Vision and Reality in the Life of the Church

Corinth: Paul's Vision of Collaboration

The letters of Paul to the community at Corinth give us a first-hand view of his theology of Christian life and his early commitment to a partnership style of ministry. They also provide us with an insight into how difficult it was to implement this vision in the everyday life of the community. We find Paul's approach to ministry outlined in passionate, even poetic language in the familiar passages of 1 Corinthians 12-14.

By way of summary, we can point to the following characteristics of Paul's understanding of ministry:

1) Each member of the community, through baptism into the one Spirit, has *charismata*—spiritual and ministerial gifts, intended for the building up of the Body of Christ.

2) These *charismata* vary greatly, but they are fundamentally equal and non-hierarchical. They are not the same as natural qualities, though they build on these in-

herent human gifts. Paul emphasizes the role of the Spirit working in all people in order to offset some of the competitive attitudes that were plaguing the Corinthian community.

3) Paul challenges the *ekklesia* of Corinth to have mutual respect for one another's gifts, so they can be freely and responsibly exercised.

4) There are several different lists of ministries in the Pauline letters (for example, 1 Cor 12:7-11; Rom 12:6-8; Eph 4:11). They vary in their order and manner of description, since they are intended to be illustrative of the various *charismata* rather than a comprehensive listing of the ways of building community.

5) In 1 Corinthians, Paul gives special attention and dignity to the charism of prophecy. A prophet, in Paul's mind, is an inspired preacher whose gift is to encourage and challenge the community to a spirit of loving service.

6) The greatest of all the *charismata* is love. Without charity as their root and foundation, the other gifts can easily be occasions for competition and divisiveness.

7) There is a practical need to order the various gifts for the common good. It is clear that some individuals and groups had been arrogant or inconsiderate in pursuing their personal agenda. Many scholars feel that Paul's attempt to order or regulate the *charismata* is the beginning of what later came to be known as "offices"—the more permanent ministerial functions by stable groups of persons in a community who lead and serve the church in some officially recognized way.

Promise and Performance: Paul's Struggle to Implement the Vision

As we have seen, women were already functioning as leaders and ministerial partners before Paul's conversion. They continued to minister independently as well as collaboratively after he emerged as a leading apostle to the Gentiles. The communities in and around Corinth had at least three women leaders in their midst: Chloe,

Prisca and Phoebe. We do not know how much their theological perspective might have influenced Paul's own pastoral approach to ministry, but it is clear that they had good working relationships with him. Even more, Paul's letters suggest that he respected these women as fellow servants of the gospel and as partners in ministry.

We can assume, therefore, that Paul concurred with the basic vision of the Antioch missionary movement. There are in fact two explicit references to the Galatians manifesto in the Corinthian letters (1 Cor 7:17-24; 12-13), indicating that Paul accepted this fundamental stance of equality as his own.

All the same, there are indications within the Pauline writings that the apostle from Tarsus was struggling with the implementation of partnership ministry. He also began to modify or at least adapt the founding vision of the missionary movement. There may be many reasons for this, the most obvious being the woundedness of people's lives and the blindness of the human condition. However clear the gospel vision of equality might have been, Paul continually encountered exploitive individuals and narrow-minded factions who acted otherwise. Some members of the communities twisted his words and distorted his teaching. Others undermined his leadership and criticized him openly during his absence. In many of the house churches there were religious extremists. Some of them advocated legalistic and inhuman forms of asceticism; others used the doctrine of the resurrection as an excuse for sexual immorality and other excesses.

We will probably never know the full reasons behind it, but it is clear that Paul began, in some areas, to shift toward a more hierarchical way of speaking about ministry (Fiorenza, p. 218 ff.). The following are some of the issues or circumstances that manifest this gradual change.

· *Marriage, Celibacy and the Parousia.* Paul, together with many other Christians in the first century, believed that the Second Coming was imminent. This expectation of "the appearance of the Lord Jesus" relativizes the meaning of everything in history and has an impact, in Paul's perspective, on human relationships. His comments in this regard are found in the seventh chapter of 1 Corinthians.

On the one hand, his words have a positive tone that affirms the equality between women and men. He stresses, for example, the emotional and sexual mutuality between husbands and wives and calls on them to live in covenantal love and shared responsibility. His advice to unmarried women also stands in contrast to the accepted androcentric dominance of Greco-Roman culture. Virginity was considered an exception, with a strong expectation that young women fulfill the social role of marriage in the patriarchal family structure. Paul's advice to virgins to remain free of the marriage bond is an invitation for them to act independently as persons. It was a direct confrontation with the values of the dominant culture.

On the other hand, Paul's comments regarding married women being "divided" in their commitment to ministry (in contrast to the "singlemindedness" of the unmarried) had a negative impact in later Christian practice. It had the implicit effect of limiting married women to the confines of the patriarchal family. It also created the impression that marriage is a "lesser state," a way of life theologically less suited to ministry. It would be interesting to know how some of the founding missionary couples responded to Paul's comments in this regard.

Paul's advice regarding celibacy and marriage must be placed in the context of the imminent expectation of the Second Coming. But even when this is taken into consideration, one can detect in his perspective a suspicion of this world and of sexuality—a suspicion soon to emerge as a serious dualism in Christian spirituality.

The Use of Patriarchal Language. Paul's language is rich and nuanced. When he wants to describe his relationship to the communities he founded, he speaks of himself in some contexts as "father." In other situations he refers to himself as "mother" and "nurse." What all of these metaphors have in common is the underlying image of the patriarchal family rather than the new community of adult disciples Jesus had envisioned. Since he himself is male, the lingering effect of Paul's language is to think of him as a "spiritual father," with the eventual effect of transferring the language and structure of the patriarchal family to the community of faith.

A similar problem arises in Paul's commentary on Genesis and the creation of woman and man (1 Cor 11:7-12). Paul's interpretation of the creation stories is less faithful to the original stance of the equality of woman and man and more dependent upon the male-dominated interpretation of the rabbis. The outcome is predictable. We are left with the impression that women are subordinate to men.

Women and Men in the Assembly. One of the most debated sections of Paul's writings is 1 Corinthians 11:2-16. We have limited information regarding the actual situation Paul is addressing in Corinth. We can only infer that he is speaking of what is or is not proper decorum when the community gathers for public prayer and worship. The problem Paul is addressing here is not related to the question of ministerial leadership. It is already clear that women and men could share equally in this role. From other passages we know that women were functioning as prophets and teachers in the community.

The issue in this particular context is related to social behavior and propriety in the assembly. Corinth, like many other cities in the Hellenic world, was strongly influenced by various eastern religious cults, which engaged in ecstatic rituals and celebrations. These services had gained a somewhat dubious reputation for going to excess in their emotional display. The general populace had apparently already begun to think of the Christian movement as one of these oriental cults. Paul is concerned about dispelling these misconceptions as well as maintaining proper order in the Christian assembly. His directives are specifically aimed at women in the congregation. It is not a mandate to cover their heads (as it is often translated), but rather to "bind up" their hair, since free flowing hair together with spontaneous talking was the pattern of the ecstatic cults.

We do not know whether or not the Corinthian community accepted Paul's advice. What we do know is that later, Deutero-Pauline writers would use issues such as these to move further toward a more patriarchal form of leadership. In the generation after Paul there is an obvious shift toward excluding women from ministerial leadership.

Patriarchal Pressures: Ministry in the Deutero-Pauline Church

In the history of any religious movement there is a normal tension between charism and office, between the spontaneous, free experience of the Spirit in individuals' lives and the stable exercise of those gifts in the wider community. The ordering of ministries and the emergence of stable offices of service within a community are necessary for its survival.

This was already the case, as we have seen, in the Pauline communities, where the circle of charisms existed alongside the emerging need to give structure and stability to these gifts. Other factors also played a role in bringing about the need for more perduring "offices" in the ministerial life of the community. The following are some of the circumstances and events that brought about the transition to a more institutionalized experience of church—what some commentators have referred to as the emergence of "early catholicism" in the pastoral letters and later writings in the New Testament.

The Delay of the Parousia

It gradually began to dawn on the Christians of the first century that the second coming of the risen Lord may not take place as they had anticipated. After the fall of Jerusalem and the spread of the good news into the Diaspora, questions arose as to how to interpret this delay theologically, and more importantly still, how to live with it creatively in Christian community. The theological interpretations varied. The Johannine tradition developed what we have come to know as "realized eschatology"—the belief that the Lord has already returned through the indwelling of the Spirit and the sacramental life of the church. Other writers, for example in 2 Peter, responded to the delay by simply intensifying the language of imminent return. Finally, the Lucan vision understands the life of the church to be the history of the Spirit in the world, combined with the belief that we are living in an extended interim, as the Word of God goes out to all the nations.

The practical effect of the delay of the Parousia was to challenge the church to enter into history by developing forms and structures that would enable it to perdure through the centuries.

The Apostolic Tradition

With the death of the original witnesses to Jesus and his resurrection, there arose the need for an "apostolic tradition"—the initial articulation of the vision of Christianity, including its central doctrines, its forms of prayer and ministry and its ethical mandates. The second generation of believers faced the demanding task of beginning to "institutionalize" the good news of Jesus.

In our time there is a tendency to be suspicious of institutions. Perhaps this is because they so frequently become depersonalized and mechanistic. On the other hand, we cannot become fully human without institutions. The word "institution" comes from the Latin term, *instare,* which literally means "to make stand." If something is of great value to human experience and we want to "hand it on" *(traditio),* we need to give it form and shape so that it can perdure from one generation to the next.

Thus, the second generation of Christians set about the task of articulating the vision and enfleshing the primordial experience of faith. Because of circumstances, which we will be addressing shortly, the initial shaping of the "tradition" began to move away from the earlier vision of a discipleship of equals and employed instead language and forms of ministry that were more patriarchal.

Heresies, Factions, Persecutions

In addition to the task of articulating its vision and practice into a tradition, the Christian movement also had to deal with other challenges to its identity and survival. Some of these came from within churches in the form of heretical movements. These factions twisted the message of the gospel to their own purposes and brought about crippling divisions. Other pressures came from without, as the gospel and those who preached it were increasingly perceived as a threat to established religious institutions and to the cultural values of the Greco-Roman world. The result was a long and painful series of persecutions carried on against Christianity.

The Tension Between Faith and Culture

At first the Christian movement was viewed as just another cult, similar to the other mystery religions which had been imported into the empire. It did not take long, however, for the counter-cultural stance of the gospel to begin having an impact in Roman society. Christians were strongly criticized for threatening the civil order through their egalitarian stance toward human relationships. It did not rest easy in the minds of the civil and religious leaders to learn that Christians felt called to confront the caste system based on race, religion, social status and gender, in order to transform it into a new experience of community. The social and political implications of baptism, as it affected slaves and their hope for freedom, threatened the very foundations of economic life. The practice of equality and partnership between women and men in marriage and ministry threatened to disrupt the patriarchal family.

At first Christians were verbally attacked for posing

a serious threat to the order of Greco-Roman society. Later this public criticism and ridicule developed into outright oppression and, in many cases, violent persecution. This tension between faith and culture was not a new phenomenon in the history of salvation. The slaves in Egypt, the prophets during the monarchy, the Israelites in exile, the "hasidim" in the Maccabbean era, all had known persecution and even martyrdom.

It is easy to forget, however, that the tension between faith and culture has a mutually transforming effect. On the one hand, persecution strengthens a community's resolve, produces heroic figures of faith, and can ultimately change the hearts of the persecuters. On the other hand, whether or not the people of faith realize it, the culture with which they wrestle also has an impact on their belief and the ways in which they celebrate it. The Hebrews conquered the land of Canaan, but in the process the Canaanite culture had a profound influence on Jewish faith and its forms of expression. In the same way, the Christians ultimately converted the Roman empire, but the gospel vision and Christianity as a way of life were also influenced and in some ways changed.

The impact of Greco-Roman culture on the Christian vision interests us here, for it reveals the gradual adaptation of the gospel vision to the political and cultural realities of the time.

The Household Codes

A great deal of research has been done in recent years regarding the Greco-Roman social and familial guidelines and the manner in which they were integrated into later New Testament writings. These "household codes," as they are known, are found in various places in the Deutero-Pauline writings and in the so-called "catholic" epistles (cf. Colossians 3:18-25; Eph 5:2-6,9; 1 Pet 2:13-3:7; 1 Tim 2:8-15, 6:1-2; Titus 2:1-10). They are a concrete example of the ways in which Christianity began to shift away from a partnership model of community and ministry to adapt itself to the values and customs of the patriarchal civil and family order.

What are the origins of the household codes? What was their function and purpose in the Hellenic culture of the time? Why were they adapted, with some minor changes, into the later New Testament writings? We will address each of these questions briefly.

Origins. Many scholars believe that the household codes have their roots in the Stoic ethical codes which had become popularized and practiced in the Greco-Roman culture of the first century. This philosophical and ethical tradition can be traced as far back as Plato, Aristotle, and perhaps even some of the pre-Socratic thinkers. Recent theories have cast some doubt upon these specifically Stoic, philosophical links, and locate their origins instead in oriental Jewish religious thought.

Structure. The household codes usually contain three pairs of exhortations concerning relationships between wives and husbands, children and fathers, slaves and masters. In each case the group that is lower on the social scale is mentioned first and urged to accept their subordinate position for the sake of good order. The actual pattern of the codes also follows a three-fold structure:

1. address: e.g. wives, children, slaves
2. exhortation: e.g. "Be submissive;" "obey;"
3. motivation: e.g. "as is fitting in the Lord."

Purpose. The ancient world was a time of radical uncertainty. Even the most politically or socially influential people had little control over the twists and turns of fate. These uncertainties included war, genocide, famine, disease, natural disasters such as earthquakes or volcanic eruptions and the possibility of mass deportation. In the face of such insecurity, ancient cultures placed a strong emphasis on the value of order and stability. Since the family with its extended network of relationships was the foundation of the rest of society and a microcosm of the state, the role of submission and obedience in the family was valued highly. The household codes articulated this value in concrete terms.

The Household Codes in the Christian Scriptures

In the face of growing criticism and persecution, the Christian communities in the late first century attempted to answer the accusations which were being leveled against them. Some of the criticism was slanderous and simply untrue. Others reflected the clash between gospel values and the Hellenic culture. In their writings the leaders of the church dissociated themselves from the other mystery cults, which met at night, practiced strange sexual rituals and often disrupted the social order. The concern to establish themselves as upright citizens who maintained stable family life was not only a defensive one. It was also motivated by the mission of evangelization and an early form of Christian apologetics.

In adapting the household codes, the church leaders changed little of their substance or meaning. They simply placed them in the context of Christian love and dedication to God. In the case of slaves, the author of Colossians and Ephesians changed the exhortation to read: "Be obedient to those who are called your masters in this world."

The motivation for integrating the household codes into the Christian scriptures is expressed well in 1 Timothy: "All slaves under the yoke must have unqualified respect for their masters, *so that the name of God and our teaching are not brought into disrepute* (6:1-2; italics ours).

Impact on Christian Life and Ministry

The gradual accommodation of partnership ministry to patriarchal cultural values had several consequences. Over the next century or more it had a positive influence in making Christianity more palatable to the civil and religious leaders of the Roman empire, resulting eventually in the conversion of the emperor Constantine. Thereby it also lessened some of the pressure of persecution and made possible the spread of the Christian gospel.

But Christianity's concern to legitimate itself as a responsible and stablizing presence in the empire also resulted in a return to patriarchal language and more hierarchical forms of ministry. This had the long term effect of setting aside the vision of Christian life as a discipleship of equals. In the later New Testament writings the role of the wandering prophets and the missionary couples is replaced by the emergence of a male-dominated leadership. In the pastoral letters we can see this taking place in the transition from prophet to *presbyteros*, from partnership to *episkopos*.

At this stage of development the terms *presbyteros* and *episkopos* are used interchangeably. They have not yet crystalized into the later meaning of "priest" and "bishop." In their terminology and style of leadership they probably represent the adaptation of the Jewish "elders," a structure that maintains a sense of collegiality and consultation, but one that is also clearly male and hierarchical in its approach to worship and ministry.

In the second century there is a further step in centralizing the offices of ministry in the classic tri-partite role of bishop, priest and deacon. The role of the bishop emerges as the unifying and stable symbol of Christian community. By the fourth century the church is gradually adopting many of the imperial structures and style of governance. Under Constantine and Theodosius, Christianity becomes a *religio*—a "civic ethos" that concentrates the meaning of religion on cultic worship. With theologians such as Cyprian, Christian ministry moves further away from a vision of partnership by returning to the levitical model of priesthood as its theological paradigm.

Conclusions

It is not our purpose here to trace the development of ministry throughout Christian history. We have focused on the tension between partnership and patriarchy, equality and hierarchy, already present in the Christian scriptures. In one sense, the pattern of the future has already taken a clear, patriarchal trajectory by the early decades of the second century. This in turn leads us to some conclusions and several questions that arise from our reflections.

1. There are two different approaches to the role of women and men in ministry in the New Testament writings. While these two traditions are not necessarily contradictory, they certainly reveal a genuine tension in their theological presuppostions.

2. The earlier of these traditions emphasizes the equality of women and men through baptism and the call to partnership ministry on behalf of the gospel of Jesus Christ. The later tradition emphasizes the need for stable, perduring offices of ministry, which are modeled on the patriarchal and hierarchical structures of the day.

3. Since both of these interpretations of ministry are contained in the canon of scripture, they can legitimately claim the inspiration of the Holy Spirit and a place of orthodoxy in Christian history.

4. Theologically, the earlier vision of ministry is rooted in the post-resurrection conviction that the disciples should model their ministry on the message and life of Jesus, even if it meant that they, like the Master, would find themselves in conflict with the cultural and religious values of their age. The later, more patriarchal approach, claims continuity with the essential message of Jesus, while realistically adapting its form and expression to make it more pastorally effective in the Greco-Roman world.

5. In practice, how can we integrate these two contrasting approaches to ministry in the contemporary church's practice? On the one hand, it appears that we ought to avoid the temptation of "primitivism"—the stance that claims that only the original, earlier practice of Christianity has legitimacy, and that any tendency toward patriarchy or hierarchy in ministry, even if this is

contained in the New Testament writings, represents a compromise of the gospel vision. On the other hand, we do have to take seriously the earlier vision and practice of partnership as an attempt to embody the life and teaching of Jesus. We also have to ask ourselves how far the gospel vision can be adapted to cultural realities without losing its integrity.

6. It is clear that the later tradition—the patriarchal and hierarchical approach—is, as one author puts it, the "historical winner." From the second century on it has been the predominant understanding and practice of ministry in the Catholic church.

7. Once again we return to the essential question: How seriously did the early Christians take the message and vision of Jesus? If, as the case certainly seems to be, they took it very seriously, then what should our contemporary response be to their vision and practice? Was the practice of ministerial partnership between women and men only a utopian ideal that was doomed from the start? Was the vision of a discipleship of equals an impossible dream which Jesus and the early church practiced, but which, in the long haul, was never intended to be lived out by other Christians?

8. The mission statement of Galatians 3:27-28 may indeed be an ideal, but it is one that needs to be taken seriously in our age. Perhaps it was too much to expect the Christian movement to reject slavery and to transform the entire social and economic structure of the Roman empire. Perhaps it was too much to expect the early church to confront the Greco-Roman culture with a consistent practice of equality between women and men in ministry.

But is it unrealistic to expect that the value of equality and inclusivity would at least continue to be held up as an ideal? Is it utopian to expect that Christianity, once it had reached a point of cultural and social influence, might use its moral leadership to recover and implement the earlier gospel vision? If anything, the evidence points to an opposite movement. As time went on, Christian theology tended to spiritualize and privatize the implications of baptism. The separation of our "spiritual lives" from "life in the world" became a given by the early Middle Ages. This stance continued to influence the church's spirituality until the emergence of Catholic social teaching at the end of the 19th century. It is ironic that the major movements to recognize the dignity of human persons in their social and political dimensions did not come from the church, but from the energy of populist movements. If anything, the church in the 18th and 19th century resisted these grassroots movements toward equality as threatening the divinely instituted order of society.

In our time the social and political movements of equality between races and genders have often had their origins outside the support or affirmation of religious groups. These egalitarian movements have in turn challenged the church to reconsider its perspective and to reach back into its tradition to recover the primordial vision of the gospel. The social teaching of the church over the last 100 years is an outcome of this return to our roots. It represents a new energy and vitality in the history of church doctrine. One of the most exciting challenges of our age is to see the church now beginning to apply this same perspective to the relationship between women and men in ministry.

7
Reclaiming the Vision
Toward Partnership in the Emerging Church

The Cosmic Egg: A Story

One morning, in a land far away, an ancient tribe awoke to discover an immense egg sitting in the center of their village. Since no one knew where the egg had come from, the people assumed it was a gift from the gods, a gift with cosmic significance. There was much excitement and lively conversation as the villagers gathered around the egg, admiring its beauty, its perfect shape and its wondrous size. Then, much to their surprise, the egg began to rumble from within, to sway and then to crack.

The sound of the cosmic egg beginning to crack evoked two different responses in the tribe. Some of the people were terrified. They either ran away and hid or demanded that the tribal leaders do something to prevent the egg from cracking further. In contrast, others watched the egg with interest and drew nearer in anticipation. "Don't run away," they shouted to the frightened ones. "Let's all move nearer so we can hear what the rumbling is telling us. Let's stay close to the egg, for if it cracks open, it might reveal a wonderful surprise!"

The Pain and the Promise of Change

The parable of the cosmic egg has no ending. Why is it left unfinished? Because it is intended to be a reflection on human experience everywhere and in every age, rather than a story about people who lived long ago and far away. The outcome of the story is being relived and rewritten each day of our lives. In the end, the focus of the story is not the egg, but our response to it. It is a parable about our stance toward change and transformation, toward the daily experience of dying and rising. The story reminds us that growth—any kind of growth—is as fearful and demanding as it is full of promise and hope.

In the deepest sense, *we* are the egg. We are the unfolding process of life, which in this universe has become conscious of itself. In the words of Teilhard, we are the "arrow of evolution," the awakening of self-consciousness and responsibility. This is true, first of all, of our personal lives and the manner in which we shape our life-journeys. Each day we must face our woundedness and embrace our gifts. Every stage of our growth involves an invitation to let go of our fears and to trust the life emerging from within us. Like the mythic tribe, we can either run from our growth in fear and denial, or enter into its mystery with trust. The difference, of course, is that we don't just watch ourselves "crack open." We are participants and shapers of life as well as its receivers.

The story of the egg also describes the stances toward change that go beyond the individual and his or her encounters with times of discontinuity. The same responses to transition and growth are found in our relational lives: in families, communities and the wider relationships of church and society.

A Church Being Born

Both the society in which we live and the church we claim as our own are "breaking open." The sound of this cracking, like the birthpangs of a new age, can be heard all around us. We hear it in the differing approaches to the gospel, in the decline of vocations to the priesthood, in the emergence of new ministries and in the perennial tension between faith and culture.

Not surprisingly, there are two different responses to this time of upheaval. Some are frightened and react with attitudes of denial or desperation. Psychologically and spiritually they are in flight. They are demanding, in effect, that the church either ignore the cracks or tape them up in an attempt to preserve the status quo.

We are not speaking here of those conservatives who reverence the past as the living link to the present and the challenge to the future. In any time of death and resurrection something must be abandoned, but also something is brought forward in creative continuity. In our time, those who adamantly resist any form of change in the church are more often motivated by fear and emotional insecurity than by reverence for past values. These voices of negativity and doom will probably continue to be heard both in the church and in our society in the coming decade. If anything, as we approach the third millennium, there will likely be increasing signs of apprehension and apocalypticism. Change is frightening and risky. Many will continue to interpret the cracks in the egg as signs of disintegration and disaster rather than the experience of new birth.

Signs of Birth, Reasons for Hope

For people of hope, on the other hand, this is an age of transformation and rebirth. This is a privileged and gifted moment to be alive. Obviously, it is a challenging and difficult era as well; a time when even the bravest among us know the dark night of fear and loneliness; a time when the most faith-filled encounter disturbing questions and doubts; but a time, nevertheless, when we are called to believe in the boundary-breaking energy of the Spirit and in our capacity, both personally and communally, to experience a new Pentecost.

For those who trust the human adventure, this is a season of hope. In the first letter of Peter the followers of

Jesus are challenged to give reasons for the hope that lies within them (1 Pet 3:15). But this task of articulating the Easter vision is not limited to the disciples who lived in the first century. Every generation of Christians has a responsibility to name the reasons and shape the words of hope. We want to respond to this challenge in our time and in our church. Where can we see the Spirit moving in our church and in our world today? What are the signs of rebirth? What direction is the renewal taking?

The following represent some of what we consider to be signs of birth in our church. They are the "reasons for our hope," especially as they relate to collaborative service, the reaffirmation of women and men as ministerial partners.

People of God: The New Metaphor for Church

To the dismay of reactionary theologians, the bishops of the Second Vatican Council did not simply reiterate the defensive posture of post-reformation ecclesiology. Instead they called for a return to the sources, a new exploration of the biblical and experiential roots from which the church was born.

The result was *Lumen Gentium*, the Dogmatic Constitution on the Church. The most striking image to emerge from that document is the title given to chapter two: "The People of God." This metaphor of the church as a pilgrim people has captured the imagination of many Catholics. It is true that this metaphor is preceded in chapter one by the image of the church as divine mystery. It is likewise complemented with several other biblical similes that recall the church as vine, Body of Christ, bride, mother, sheepfold, cultivated field, building, temple and communion of saints. It is also true that in chapter three of *Lumen Gentium* we are reminded of the hierarchical nature of the church.

All the same, the mobilizing metaphor of this council document remains the image of church as a community of faith in history. The result has been a revolution in Catholic consciousness that is stronger than our words and deeper than our symbols. It is a shift from understanding the church primarily as a hierarchical institution to experiencing it as a community of disciples. It is a way of recognizing the primordial dignity of baptism as the basis for all mission and ministry. Not least of all, it is the first step toward reclaiming the church as a partnership of love and a discipleship of equals.

Collegiality: The New Style of Leadership

The Second Vatican Council called the church to a new form of listening and leadership. The term that emerged from the council to describe this new attitude of consultation is "collegiality." In its original setting, collegiality was used to describe the relationship the bishops have with the pope in their joint role as teachers and leaders of the church. The pattern of this relationship is not based on the model of king and subjects, or teacher and students, but that of a *collegium* —a leader in a community of leaders, a shepherd among fellow shepherds with shared reponsibility for proclaiming the gospel and building up the Body of Christ.

In the wake of the council a significant pastoral development has taken place with regard to collegiality. What was spoken of as a relationship between pope and bishops has been extended as an attitude or manner of communication in the wider church. The development of national conferences of bishops and the regular meeting of the synod of bishops in Rome reflects this wider sense of collegiality on the episcopal level.

In the United States, the stance of collegiality has had a profound impact on the way in which the American bishops exercise their teaching role. In a series of ground-breaking pastoral letters ("The Challenge of Peace," 1983; "Economic Justice for All," 1986; "Partners in the Mystery of Redemption," First Draft, 1988), the United States bishops have adopted a new listening and dialogical approach in their role as pastoral leaders. They are addressing some of the most significant issues in today's church and society—peace, economic justice, the equality of women and men—with a consistent commitment to dialogue at the grassroots.

But it is especially in local communities—parishes, religious congregations, health care institutions, and justice and peace ministries—that the style of consultation and shared responsibility has had the most impact. Here, in the everyday life of the church, the theological vision of collegiality is becoming a contemporary version of "partnership ministry." Collegiality is being translated into a commitment to shared responsibility in parish councils and diocesan administrations. It is taking the form of team ministry on parish staffs and in religious communities.

The movement toward a more collegial church is not without its pain, its fear and its resistance. Not all pastoral leaders believe in partnership and shared responsibility. One is left wondering at times whether some of the bishops and Vatican leaders do not feel threatened by the very vision they articulated at Vatican II. Even given these fears, however, few can deny that a new energy of the Spirit has been released at the level of the people. It is difficult to ignore the growing awareness of women and men as collaborators in the emerging church.

Liberation Theology: Confronting the Structures of Oppression

From the marginated peoples of Latin America and other Third World countries, another theological movement of solidarity and social transformation has emerged. Rooted in the scriptures and flowing from the contemporary church's "option for the poor," this theological perspective reflects the practical implications of living the gospel in our time. In one sense liberation theology is a contemporary version of Jesus' metaphor for ministry and the reign of God. It challenges the church to move beyond "temple" (cultic worship) and "torah" (rules or external observance) to the "festive table" of equality and inclusiveness among all peoples. Even before the church is *for* the poor or *with* the poor, it is first of all a church *from* the poor.

The implications of liberation theology are strongly affecting the global stance of the church toward human rights and the movements toward democracy. It also speaks directly to the call for equality between women and men and the need for ministerial partnership in families, small communities and church structures at all levels.

Feminism: A Commitment to Equality and Inclusivity

In our culture, and perhaps even more so in our church, the emergence of the feminist movement was greeted with both skepticism and apprehension. Significant numbers of people, including many women, tended to dismiss the movement as being too radical in its politics and too dangerous in its approach to traditional family and religious values. Initially, some of these fears may have been justified, since most social movements begin out of a vortex of frustration, anger and even revolution. It is becoming increasingly clear, however, that the feminist movement has touched something deep and authentic in the growth of human community and personhood. It is confronting the centuries-old domination of patriarchal thinking and structures in our culture and our social institutions. It is part of the rising consciousness of human rights around the world. It speaks of the essential dignity of every human person and the consequent equality of women and men, themes articulated by *Pacem in Terris*, *Gaudium et Spes*, and most of the other major church statements on social justice in this century.

Authentic feminism involves more than the quest for gender equality. It is a confrontation with any form of exploitation or arrogance of one human being toward another; it is ultimately a vision of healing and reconciliation between genders, races, ethnic groups and social classes.

The Emergence of Small Christian Communities

Another phenomenon speaks of hope and the recovery of collaborative ministry in the church. Throughout the world, in different cultural and social settings, small communities of Christians are gathering in prayer, reflection and transformative service. In their book *Dangerous Memories: House Churches and Our American Story* Bernard J. Lee and Michael A. Cowan profile the background and implications of this movement in the global church. For the most part this "regathering of the churches" has arisen at the initiative of the people rather than at the insistence of the hierarchical church. In Latin America these gatherings are referred to as "base communities" *(communidades de base)*; in Africa and Asia they are sometimes called "small Christian communities"; in Europe and in North America they are usually characterized as "intentional communities," since they include a wide range of relational experiences such as prayer groups, Catholic Worker Houses, covenant communities, alternative parishes, as well as groups arising from Cursillo, Marriage Encounter, Renew and the separated and divorced ministry.

This global movement toward small Christian communities reflects a powerful movement of the Spirit, a surprising source of energy and renewed faith, which was neither expected nor planned by the institutional church. In many ways they represent a contemporary return to the house-churches of the first century. They tend to emphasize mutuality in relationships, a spirit of prayerful discernment, a commitment to social transformation and a collaborative style of leadership. They embody the image of a "circle of charisms," the sharing of ministerial gifts in the energy of partnership.

A Time of Transition: Reasons for Concern

The above represent some of the reasons for trusting the direction of the Spirit and the renewal of partnership ministry in our time. They give us solid reasons for our hope. But hope is not the same as blind optimism. If there are reasons for hope, there is also ample room for concern. Growth and renewal seldom occur without ambiguity and pain; obviously, they never take place in a vacuum. In a time of transition the ambiguity and the tension are more pronounced. The level of anxiety is heightened; the currents of confusion can sometimes feel like a swirling vortex that threatens to engulf the energies of renewal.

In the post-Vatican II church this sense of psychic and pastoral vertigo has been a familiar, if disconcerting experience. We sometimes feel that we are walking on the edge of chaos; a fear that our best efforts at reform will only plunge us into the abyss; an anxiety that if we let go of that which is apparently stable and secure, we will lose everything we claim as essential to our tradition.

In the face of this insecurity, we are nevertheless called to "stand in the breach." We are challenged to carry forward the vision of renewal in the face of upheaval and conflict. We know both the peril and the promise of the emerging church. The sounds of the "cracking egg" are all around us: differing theological approaches divide communities and paralyze their sense of mission; the search for fads or easy relevance is sometimes substituted for the authentic recovery of the tradition; the renewed vision of sacramental theology encounters resistance and the lingering fears of change; a biblical centered catechetics struggles to put down roots in unfamiliar and even unfriendly soil. The new wine does not rest well in old wineskins.

Even when the emerging vision is relatively clear, as in the need for collegial structures and consultative forms of leadership, the actual implementation of that vision frequently falters and then dissipates its energy. This can happen in many different ways: a bishop who speaks the rhetoric of shared responsibility, but acts unilaterally; a newly appointed pastor who sidetracks or reverses years of planning and decision making in a local congregation; boards and parish staffs who, willfully or out of necessity, compete with each other for limited financial resources; lay leaders who are invited into ministry but are not provided the formation, the support or the resources to carry out their work; professionally trained women who are not taken seriously in their ministerial roles; priests with years of effective pastoral experience who are devalued or pushed aside. These are only a few of the ways in which the vision of partnership can flounder and fail.

Thus the challenge of renewal is also the call to Christian realism, the recognition that change comes slowly and painfully. The transformation of attitudes and patterns of behavior takes time, patient endurance and courage. "Vatican II," writes Karl Rahner, "is the beginning of a beginning." Whatever the vision of the contemporary church regarding new forms of collaboration, the implementation of this vision is a formidable task. Patriarchal structures of authority have been in place for a long time. They will not give way easily to a partnership style of leadership. Even when there is a willingness to shift from an authoritarian manner, there is not always the competency or the capacity to make a collegial style effective.

Implementing the Vision: The Challenge Before Us

Despite our fears and uncertainties, the work of renewal must go on. We are living in a time of overlap, when the attitudes and structures of the past still influence the work of the present. In the church, as in the wider society, there are a plurality of approaches to human leadership and community. For the sake of discussion, we are reducing this diversity to three fundamental stances toward authority and leadership style. We are referring to them as (1) the *corporate* model; (2) the *family* model; and (3) the *collaborative* model. These differing and sometimes contrary stances are often operative in the same setting under different circumstances. Some pastors or pastoral leaders are committed to one, while their staff and parish council may be operating out of the assumptions and expectations of another. In reality, none of them exists in a pure state. Our hope is that in understanding the dynamics of each one, we can move more effectively toward the partnership model we feel is at the heart of the gospel.

The Corporate Model

In the '60s an article appeared in *Fortune* magazine that claimed that the two most successful corporations in the world, from the viewpoint of efficient management, were General Motors and the Roman Catholic Church. It is doubtful that this same claim would be made today, but the setting in which it was articulated gives us an important clue to the public image the church conveyed to the world just prior to the Second Vatican Council.

One could conceivably argue that the word "corporate" has biblical roots. After all, the Latin term *corpus* means "body" as in *Corpus Christi*, one of the earliest names for the Eucharist and one of Paul's metaphors for the church. Paul's use of "Body of Christ" for the church also emphasizes the dynamic interrelationship of the various parts of the body and the need for them to operate harmoniously for the sake of the whole living organism.

Whatever the biblical connotations might be, that meaning is not operative here. We are focusing instead on the meaning of "corporate" as descriptive of the management style of large business organizations. The corporate model has many advantages. It is designed for efficiency and productivity; it has clear, hierarchical lines of authority; it is a system of communication and subordination that leaves little room for ambiguity or misunderstanding. It is designed, as the business world is fond of saying, to "get the job done." The virtues extolled in the corporate model are obedience and orthodoxy. When we transfer the corporate model from the business world to religious organizations, we have the classic image of the church in the '40s and '50s of this century.

The disadvantage of the corporate approach is that it tends to be cold, dispassionate, impersonal and, at times, uncaring. The vision and the direction come from the top management. The rest of the workers do not have a feeling of participation or personal ownership in the mission of the organization. They simply carry out the policies and mandates of the leaders. As a result, the corporate model does not foster a strong emphasis on creativity or personal initiative.

The *Fortune* article rated the church among the best corporate models in the world because it had a genuine respect for the church's operational efficiency and doctrinal clarity. Some aspects of the church's life still function along these lines. Despite the emphasis on collegiality in today's church, we can find the corporate stance to leadership operating in some Vatican congregations, several chancery offices and not a few parishes.

Since the '60s the corporate model has fallen upon difficult times, both in its public image and in its reputation for effectiveness. Ironically, this is true first of all in the business world itself. It has become clear that a participatory style of management actually enhances motivation and the quality of production. From small businesses to multi-national corporations the emphasis now is on shared planning, worker initiative, and employee ownership.

The Family Model

In some instances the reaction against the corporate model has led to experimenting with a more familial style of leadership and ministry. This phenomenon has not been as likely to appear in businesses or in the hierarchy of the church, as it has in local parishes. Corporations have become more open to the benefits of participatory management and the bishops are emphasizing a collegial approach to church governance, but in both cases it is still within a clearly hierarchical framework.

On the level of parish life, however, many have tried to establish the open, warm setting of the family as a way of relating to one another. Many pastors who had been trained in the corporate form of leadership and who were used to being the hierarchical leader have tried to be one with their staffs and parishioners. Where there were formalities and deference, they have substituted informality and and a more casual approach to decision making.

The positive side of the family model is rather obvious: It breaks down previous barriers of status and privilege; it is far more compassionate and personal; it invites people into the warmth of community. It changes both the style and the language of interrelating: St. Leo's "congregation" becomes St. Leo's "parish family." Social gatherings, ranging from coffee and doughnuts after Sunday liturgy to annual spaghetti dinners, become an essential part of the church's life and ministry.

The family model appears to embody the high value contemporary pastoral theology places on *koinonia*—the building up of a spirit of *community*. In many parishes, particularly those that have had strong roots in a neighborhood or ethnic group, this sense of solidarity already existed among the people even under the corporate model of leadership previous to Vatican II. The renewal has simply affirmed and celebrated this community bond.

As attractive as the family model is for parish life, it has its limitations and potential problems. This is especially true when one tries to adopt it as a style of pastoral leadership. If the corporate model is too hierarchical, dispassionate and unilateral, the family model can easily become confusing in its expectations and blurred in its ministerial focus. When *koinonia* is understood as a kind of in-house "coziness," the focus of real ministry can easily become obscured. Whatever is gained in warmth and informality can be lost in terms of effective service to the wider community. Worse yet, painful situations of conflict and misunderstanding can arise because of the absence of job descriptions, clear lines of accountability and effective methods of evaluation.

If the expectation of parish leadership is to function as a family, the results may be more dysfunctional than productive of genuine *koinonia* and *diakonia*. Ministers can easily project their earlier family roles and behavior patterns into the context of pastoral leadership. For instance adults who come from alcoholic families or other dysfunctional backgrounds will tend to function in similar patterns on parish staffs: The rescuer will adopt the role of rescuer; the emotionally needy will expect to be taken care of; the rebel will ignite brush fires; the passive will withdraw. In psychological language this is a kind of *transference* —the proclivity to respond to others in our adult life out of the behavioral patterns of our childhood and growing up. Some transference is an inevitable part of all our relationships. An awareness of it will enable us to channel our energy into deeper understanding and mutuality. However, if the setting for adult relationships is either implicitly or explicitly that of a family model, the problematic side of transference will become all the more evident.

The Collaborative Model

Effective ministry in today's world needs to go beyond the corporate and family models of leadership to authentic collaboration. What do we mean by collaboration? What is distinctive about the partnership model of ministry? What sets it apart in practice from the corporate and family models?

In the first place, both the corporate and family models presuppose a hierarchical structure, whether it is the clear employer-employee relationship of the former, or the more subtle father-and-his-family relationship of the latter. In the long run neither of them makes possible an authentic "community of disciples." Neither of them nurtures the mature, adult relationship in which mutuality and shared responsibility become the basis for generative ministry.

Collaboration also calls us to a different level of maturity and mutuality than the family setting. The intimacy of the family is, on one level, more intense and transparent; it presupposes the normal dependence of children on their parents in the process of their growth toward maturity. Compared to an intentional community of adults, the family has a different set of emotional and psychic boundaries. On another level, however, the commitment to mutuality is even greater in the collaborative model than in family life, especially now that the male domination of ministry is giving way to partnership with women. Collaboration or partnership ministry demands a greater depth of self-awareness; it calls us to a level of intimacy that is less dependent and more self-disclosive; it requires a commitment to emotional honesty and the willingness to deal with conflict maturely. In short, collaboration presupposes a level of integration and maturity which will make possible a true "circle of charisms."

A third characteristic of collaboration is the search to recover the true meaning of *authority*. There is a note of irony in this assertion, since the critics of collegiality frequently maintain that shared responsibility is, in effect, a breakdown of traditional authority. There is an essential difference, however, between *authoritarianism* and healthy *authority*. The first is a stance of control and abasement; the second is the creative release of human energy for the sake of building community. The word *authority* comes from the Latin, *auctoritas*, which can best be translated as "enabling growth" or "expanding life." Authority is the creative capacity to call forth the vision and gifts of people; it is inviting rather than controlling, nurturing rather than constrictive.

The renewal taking place in our midst is not a rejection of authority, but a search for authentic leadership. If religious life as we have known it is coming to an end, it is not because human beings lack spiritual aspirations, but because, as Eugene C. Kennedy has pointed out, it can no longer function as a male-dominated, authoritarian culture. The structures of parish community, priesthood, career ministries and religious life are being transformed by the recovery of partnership ministry.

Finally, collaboration as a model of ministry is more "centrifugal" than the family pattern; its ultimate aim is the mobilization of energy that will enable the wider community to claim their role as a life-giving presence in the world. Paul referred to the women and men who worked with him as *synergoi,* a word which literally means "energy sharers" or "ministry partners." Our English word "collaborate" is a derivative from the Latin translation of *synergos* —it attempts, linguistically and theologically, to recover this early biblical vision of ministerial partnership. The collaborative model combines the need for mutuality with a commitment to service; it includes dimensions of mutual support, friendship, celebration and shared prayer, but its underlying energy is outward. *Koinonia* becomes *diaconia.*

8
Male-Female Differences
Behavioral Sciences and the Patriarchal Assumption

The early Christians found a direction for their lives and work in the dramatic ministry manifesto of Galatians 3. Its bold proclamations urged them to eliminate slavery and oppression, to be inclusive toward all peoples, and to live in equality as women and men.

We have already reflected on the role of this manifesto in the early church. We turn now to one particular aspect of this pastoral vision, an element central to its theology and values. Galatians 3:28 is not only a declaration regarding the equality between slaves and free, Gentiles and Jews, males and females. It also makes a statement about the risen Christ. In the person of the risen Christ we find the ultimate source of a humanity that belongs to everyone.

Although popular religious understanding tends to identify the Jesus of history with the risen Christ, this fusion can obscure some important realities. While there certainly is continuity between the Jesus of history and the risen Christ, the Jesus of history was born into and confined by a male body. As such, he was limited to the expression of only one dimension of humanness—a male reality. Because of the limitations of the human condition, the Jesus of history could not fully represent both sexes at the same time. Although we believe that he achieved complete integration as a man, his integration does not imply release from the limitations of gender. In fact, the early Christian community at Philippi took care to emphasize that Jesus did not attempt to use his divinity to escape from the limitations of his humanity (Phil 2:6-7). Because the Jesus of history lived out of a male perspective he could not know female experience from the inside, nor could he fully represent it.

In the minds of the Galatian community, the expression "in Christ . . . there is neither male nor female" did not refer to the Jesus of history but to the risen Christ. In other words, it would not be consistent with the theology of Galatians 3 to say that in Jesus of Nazareth there is neither male nor female. In fact, the opposite was true. In Jesus of Nazareth, there was male and not female. Likewise, in Jesus of Nazareth, there was Jew, not Greek and free, not slave.

In contrast, the risen Christ has transcended the limitations of cultural boundaries, social status and sexual categories. We do not regard Jesus as the risen Lord who is exclusively Jewish. For some reason, Christians have allowed the confines of Jesus' historical race and cultural heritage to fade into the background. We don't need the risen Lord to remain Jewish. But we do seem to need him to remain male. Yet, the same realities that apply to ethnic and racial boundaries apply to sexual categories as well. The risen Christ can no longer be confined to male biology, male experience or a male perspective. We do not know how sexuality is expressed in the resurrected state. But we do know that it can only be a liberating rather than a confining experience. When we think of the Christ of the resurrection, therefore, we should not think of Jesus the risen male, but rather, of Jesus who has moved beyond the limitations of sexual categories and become fully able to know both male and female realities. The risen Christ is significant because of transformed humanness, not resurrected maleness.

The Galatians Manifesto vs. Patriarchy

The ministry manifesto is a powerful statement about the vision of partnership. It invites us to think outside of the usual categories that separate and divide people. But as much as it was an essential aspect of early Christian belief and practice, the manifesto progressively lost influence as the church moved forward in history. The notion that the risen Christ was not limited to a male human nature did not find easy acceptance in a patriarchal society. It has not found easy acceptance in these seemingly theologically enlightened times. Patriarchy prefers maleness. It needs a male savior. It needs him to stay male. And it needs males to represent him.

The ministry manifesto of Galatians 3 announces a radical equality among males and females and proclaims the visible manifestation of that equality to be central to one's baptismal commitment. Patriarchy, too, has a manifesto of sorts. It announces that maleness, not humanness, is the normative model for society and proclaims that females can only be defined in relationship to males.

Patriarchy was deeply entrenched in the Hebrew society. It was a society that took for granted the patriarchal assumption, namely, that male experience is normative for all people. It was comfortable allowing male pronouns, male images and male metaphors to express the reality of females. It was insistent that its God be male. The maleness of the Judeo-Christian God says more about patriarchy than it says about the nature of the divine.

Patriarchy was not only embedded in the religious structures of Judaism. It was also part of the Greco-Roman world in which the bible was written and in which the earliest Christians struggled to preach the liberating word of God. Patriarchy governed the relations between the sexes and dictated that males were superior to females. The ministry manifesto stood in stark contrast to the religious and social attitudes of the day. It challenged the foundations of both. It is not surprising that it found survival difficult.

Patriarchy and the Behavioral Sciences

The vision of male-female partnership did not find it any easier to survive in modern times. Even though the behavioral sciences began, in their initial stages, in opposition to the religious structures of the day, they did not question the fundamental patriarchal premise on which religion rested. Rather, science accepted the patriarchal assumption and continued to view male experience as normative.

The new science of psychology was eyed with suspicion by the institutional church. But despite their mutual animosity, they both shared a common presumption. Ironically, Freud's contention that "anatomy is destiny" fit neatly into the religious scheme of things. Perhaps without realizing it, the church had set the stage for accepting a psychology that taught that a woman's possession of a uterus determined her role and defined her possibilities.

However unwittingly, religious patriarchy and Freudian psychology cooperated with each other in creating a deeper sense of division between women and men. When Adam and Eve tasted the forbidden fruit, patriarchy decreed that it was Eve's fault. Her punishment included pain in childbirth. Freud expanded her punishment beyond the birthing process and extended it to the status of destiny. The essence of his idea had already been articulated by the church fathers who had gone before him. Patriarchy, Freud and the institutional church all have at least one thing in common: They are males deciding for females. And their decisions reflect the bias that woman's reality is best defined by her biology, by what her body can do.

To this day, church documents speak about the "special role of women" as mothers. No mention is made of the contribution a woman might make to the development of church doctrine regarding the Eucharist—a contribution rendered unique because her body equips her to understand some things about feeding that a man could never know in the same way. We simply don't hear the institutional church emphasizing the "special role of women" as theologians.

The ecclesiastical leadership acknowledges a woman's brain insofar as it gives vital assistance to her primary childrearing function, but it ignores this same source of insight when it comes to matters of theological and biblical research, formulation of church doctrine, interpretation of scripture, preparation and delivery of homilies and institutional church leadership.

As long as woman's role as mother is stressed and associated with housekeeping and child care, much of her wisdom on behalf of the wider community can easily be lost. Trapped between hamburger helper and trips to the pediatrician, the things she instinctively knows about the sacrament of life cannot find their way into theology books. It seems ironic that the very people most closely associated with giving birth, nurturing life and teaching the young are not allowed to preside at the sacraments that ritualize these moments spiritually.

Our purpose is not to minimize the importance of motherhood, or to suggest that women who choose to combine full-time parenting and homemaking are in some way limited. We do, however, want to stress the following:

1. *Anatomy is not destiny.* Just because a woman has a uterus, and can have babies, this does not define her primary role in life. No single bodily organ is responsible for summing up one's chief reason for existing. She also has a brain, a brain that can be as vital to the collective wisdom of church and society as it is to the raising of children. Men have testicles which produce semen, which, in turn enable them to sire children. The institutional church does not use this as an argument for men's "primary role as fathers."

2. *Women's experience is sacramental.* Their bodies not only equip them to carry, birth and nurse chil-

dren; they also invite them to *reflect* on these experiences, to deepen their understanding of these life processes and apply their insights to the broader worlds of religious symbol, sacramental expression, national and international politics, ecology and world peace. It has been said that if the women who have endured labor to bring forth a child were in charge of the world, the bloody slaughter of war would soon come to an end.

3. *Males also participate in the creation of a child.* They ought to share as much of the responsibility for nurturing, teaching and caring for their children as do women. Any division of labor that relegates males solely to the outside world of work and societal leadership, and women to the kitchen and the nursery is, in the long run, a disservice to both women and men. Women are not genetically predisposed to changing diapers and men will not suffer chromosome damage by watching "Sesame Street" with a two year old.

4. *As a community of faith, the church must witness to partnership.* An ecclesial leadership that continually stresses the special role of women as mothers and does not equally stress the special role of men as fathers, and the unique contribution of both to theology, is operating by a double standard and is promoting sexism.

Anima and Animus: Jung's Attempt to Restore Partnership

Even though he had initially been a follower of Freud, Swiss psychologist Carl Jung later departed from his former mentor in several significant areas. One of the major points of difference is Jung's approach to male-female psychology. Fueled by a belief that women and men were designed to complement rather than oppose each other, Jung set out to describe ways in which this could be experientially verified. Much of the thinking about male-female psychology that has dominated contemporary society has come from Jung's research and writing.

In its popular form, Jung's thinking suggests that each person has a built-in set of characteristics that are integral to their gender: "feminine" characteristics for the female and "masculine" characteristics for the male. In addition, each person has a less visible personality component made up of the traits of the opposite sex. According to Jung, the feminine part of a man's personality is called the "anima" and the masculine part of a woman's personality is the "animus." Growth toward human wholeness requires the male to access and integrate his "anima" into his personality and the female to do the same with her "animus." The balanced person, in Jung's framework, is the male who has a strong masculinity but who is aware of and able to manifest his feminine side, or a female who exemplifies femininity but who also has a clear sense of her masculine side.

Although varying adjectives are used today to describe Jung's masculine and feminine traits, in general they consist of the following:

FEMININE TRAITS	MASCULINE TRAITS
Nurturance	Responsibility
Receptivity	Assertiveness
Passivity	Activity
Subjectivity	Objectivity
Emotionality	Rationality
Intuition	Logic
Dependence	Independence

Jung believed that the feminine traits revolved around a woman's instinct to seek belonging and relating, while the masculine ones described a man's innate drive toward autonomy. Individuals who were able to appropriately integrate both sets of traits into their personalities were considered *androgynous*.

Androgyny is a term derived from two Greek words—*andro* (male) and *gyne* (female). In Jung's day, the androgynous male was clearly masculine, but comfortable calling forth his feminine traits when the situation called for them. Likewise, the androgynous female exemplified femininity, but could call upon her "animus" when she needed it.

Jung's earlier use of the term "androgyny" has undergone considerable development, so that today it is used in a variety of ways to describe a variety of conditions. To many, androgyny is the goal of a truly non-sexist society and describes a condition in which the traits of women and men are not rigidly assigned. People are free to be themselves and to express whatever traits are instinctive to them. They do not have to be overly concerned about role conformity. In this view, a man can cry without being considered feminine and a woman can choose to be a logger without society describing her as "too masculine." Accordingly, the "macho" man and the sweet, helpless woman would vanish as common images of males and females.

Some descriptions of androgyny are more radical. They refer to a purposeful obliteration of any visible distinctions between the sexes. These, however, seem to reflect the views of a small minority.

Scientifically, androgynous individuals are defined according to the way they score on measures of masculinity and femininity, as suggested by Jung's list of traits. An androgynous person is one who *scores high on measures of both masculinity and femininity*. In other words, the androgynous person is one who is both assertive and receptive, nurturant and responsible, independent yet in need of support from relationships. He or she is role flexible and can behave according to the needs of a situation rather than the dictates of a stereotype. Studies have shown that androgynous individuals have higher levels of psychological adjustment than do the tightly "masculine" men and strictly "feminine" women of Jung's era. They tend, as a group, to look healthier than do people who are rigidly role bound.

A CRITIQUE OF JUNG'S MASCULINE-FEMININE PSYCHOLOGY

While much popular spirituality has been built upon Jung's analysis of male-female differences, contemporary psychology and theology has brought it under increasing scrutiny. Some obvious problems with his trait theory include the following:

—— its poor ability to describe accurately a large segment of the male-female population;

—— its evolution into stereotypes weighted negatively against women;

—— its lack of emphasis on healthy human traits that are not gender specific;

—— its tendency to associate masculinity and femininity with physical appearance;

—— its use of dichotomous (either-or) thinking.

Because the concepts of masculinity and femininity, as they have evolved from Jung's original ideas, are so influential in our society and church, we want to examine each of these problem areas in greater detail. Even though Jung's original intention was to bridge the gender gap, and to re-win some sense of complementarity between males and females, the actual results have fallen short of that ideal. Some would even say that the trait theory that divided males and females into different categories has actually sabotaged the vision of partnership.

Descriptive Accuracy

Many men in our society experience themselves as much more nurturant, compassionate, gentle and able to express emotion than Jung's theory would say is natural for males. These men, irrespective of their sexual orientation, simply do not have a dominant supply of Jung's "masculine" characteristics.

The same can be said of women who find themselves more naturally assertive, more oriented toward logical thinking, and more inclined to be analytical than their more "feminine" sisters. When Jung's descriptions of "masculinity" and "femininity" don't fit the individual, the tendency is to think that something is wrong with the person who doesn't match the stereotype, rather than examine the stereotype itself for accuracy. In these instances, it is not uncommon for individuals to find themselves harshly judged or looked down upon because they do not embody the characteristics of the appropriate masculine or feminine category.

Stereotyping That Is Negative Toward Women

A closer look at Jung's original descriptions of male and female traits reveals a negative weighting toward women. Some have even observed that Jung's descriptions of masculinity form the skeleton of society's definitions of adult maturity (responsible, assertive, independent), while his traits associated with femininity constitute some of the primary characteristics of mental instability (dependent, emotional, passive). Even though Jung himself may not have intended this, the descriptions of "neurotic" behavior found in many mental health writings, including the DSM III categories used by the psychiatric community in the 1980s, provide a striking parallel to Jung's traits of femininity.

A woman who embodies Jung's definition of the feminine, but is not in touch with her "animus," would be a truly pathetic person. Her extreme "femininity" might win her a long-term spot on a psychiatric couch. On the other hand, a man who exemplifies masculinity, but is unaware of his "anima," would perhaps be considered too "macho" by some standards, but in our culture he would not be significantly hindered by these traits. A "Rambo" of sorts, he would find ready acceptance by a large segment of society.

Masculine, Feminine or Human?

Recent psychological insights into what it means to be a healthy adult are rendering Jung's masculine-feminine trait theory somewhat obsolete. Some of what is best in his definitions of both masculinity and femininity—the capacity to care, to feel, to be gentle and sensitive, to be assertive, articulate and self-possessed—are increasingly regarded not as qualities that are innately more characteristic of one sex or the other, but rather, as traits specific to psychological wholeness in both sexes.

A man who is warm and sensitive is not "discovering his feminine side" but is simply being more authentically human. Sensitivity is a *human* trait, not a feminine trait. A woman who speaks more decisively than she did in the past is not "recovering her animus" but growing toward greater integration as a human person. Assertiveness is a *human* trait, not a masculine one.

Masculinity and Femininity as Physical Appearance

While Jung's original intention was to identify personality traits in males and females, society has grown accustomed to using the terms masculine and feminine to refer to someone's physical appearance. Femininity is not only associated with nurturance and emotion, but also with ruffles, pierced ears, a soft voice and slender curves. The unfortunate woman who is large-boned, doesn't wear make-up, has short, straight hair and prefers slacks to dresses is considered masculine or unfeminine by a large segment of people.

The man who has a slight body build, small facial features, and moves gracefully, experiences a similar judgment at the hands of an often harsh society. Eyebrows will be raised and jokes will be whispered at his effeminate appearance.

Many women and men in our society suffer a quiet agony because of a body shape they did not choose. It was not Jung's intention to have the terms masculine and feminine so closely associated with the externals of peoples' physical appearance. Nor was it his intention to use these categories to hurt or insult those whose bodies did not match a psychological ideal. However, in many instances that does seem to be what has happened.

This unfortunate stress on physical appearance as an indicator of masculinity and femininity has forced many individuals to seek desperate alternatives. They take steroids, endure exercise past the point of health, have plastic surgery, consume diet pills and become anorexic, often just to make themselves look more feminine or more masculine. While most healthy individuals ignore societal pressure to conform to physical externals, for many, the pressure to fit in is great. As long as we make big biceps and a hairy chest the litmus test for true masculinity, we will continue to raise generations of men who are more inclined to engage in fist fights than in self-disclosure. Similarly, unless we stop giving women the message that willowy legs and a nineteen inch waistline qualify them as feminine, many women will continue to live as though anatomy really is destiny. To be sure, many women and men don't care if they achieve the masculine and feminine appearance so coveted by much of society. But others will suffer lifelong lowering of self-esteem for failing to measure up.

Masculine and Feminine: Examples of Dichotomous Thinking

Drawing attention to trait differences in males and females, as opposed to emphasizing the similarities in their shared humanness, forces society to focus on separation rather than union. The "either-or" thinking characterized by describing reality in polar opposites has a subtle but pronounced effect on the mind. It anesthetizes us into forming concepts more comfortable with division than with connection. When we divide reality into "right and wrong," "black and white," "night and day," we become comfortable with misjudging the in-betweens. We forget about gray and we miss the twilight. When we assign masculine and feminine labels to traits that ought to characterize all healthy people, we lose sight of what is most deeply human.

Dichotomous thinking involves the polarization of categories into opposites that, more often than not, are mutually exclusive. In order to keep the categories clear, we need to keep them separated by strict definitions. For example, if a little girl prefers climbing trees to playing house, she is a "tomboy." She is operating outside of the definition of femininity. If she does not fit the feminine category, there is only one other—the masculine category. There is no in-between. Even very young children know they cannot live outside the appropriate category for long without being labeled negatively. While this way of structuring reality might sound innocent enough when it comes to climbing trees, in the long run it underlies the evils of racism, classism, sexism, moralism and militarism.

Polarization rarely exists without its partner, *hierarchicalization*—the tendency to assign different values to the polar opposites. One pole becomes higher, the other is lower. One is better, the other is worse. One has more value, the other has less value. We have seen how this has happened with the polar opposites of masculine traits and feminine traits. Neither dichotomous thinking nor hierarchicalization of reality bear much resemblance to a vision that described male and female as bone of each other's bone, flesh of each other's flesh.

Jung and Patriarchy

Jung tried to recover something of the partnership vision when he developed his masculine-feminine trait theory. In a sense, he reoriented males and females toward each other. He invited them to rediscover the fundamental connection that is part of their nature.

Unfortunately, Jung developed his theories about male-female psychology within the confines of a patriarchal world-view. Understandably, he was not able to think beyond the scientific mindset of his day. Patriarchy thinks dichotomously and so did Jung. Even while he attempted to describe complementarity between males and females, he did so by using the style of thinking characteristic of patriarchy. He used the categories of polar opposites: masculine-feminine; assertive-receptive; emotional-intellectual; intuitive-analytical.

Dichotomous thinking is more common than most of us realize. It virtually invades our way of reasoning, even when we do not need it, or would not want it if we realized it was operative. In light of this, it will be helpful to examine this approach to reality further.

Dichotomous Thinking: When It Is Healthy and When It Is Not

We are learning more today about the underlying causes of polarized or dichotomous thinking. Generally, two groups of people regularly engage in it: young children and dysfunctional adults.

Little children think dichotomously as a stage of their cognitive development. In order to understand reality and to begin to form concepts, they need to divide reality into opposites. For example, in learning how to understand the reality "dog," a young child learns what it is not. It is not a cat. It is not a horse. It does not go "moo." The child gradually learns what comprises the entity "dog" by separating out everything that is not dog. Only after these basic separations have occurred can the child begin to put things together and understand concepts such as "animal." In this stage of cognitive development, the differences between things become extremely important and temporarily over-emphasized.

The child learns the concept of gender identity in the same way. A little girl comes to know what "girl" is by separating out everything that is "boy." Girls play with dolls, boys play with trucks. Girls wear dresses, boys wear pants. Girls have a clitoris, boys have a penis (or worse, boys have a penis, girls do not!). This tendency in young children to divide "boyness" and "girlness" into polar opposites seems to be a necessary stage in enabling them to come to a clear sense of gender identity.

From a psychological perspective, therefore, dichotomous thinking is a *stage*. It is a stage characteristic of *young children* and is, or ought to be, temporary. Children who are allowed gender specific play will be more apt to have a strong sense of gender identity (a sense of their maleness or femaleness) and will be more able to abandon the cognitive polarization of the sexes as they continue to develop. Studies have shown that children who have a secure sense of gender identity become more androgynous (less gender rigid) as adults.

The second group of individuals who tend to think dichotomously are those raised in dysfunctional families. The dysfunction can come from alcoholism, parental loss through divorce or death, or from any other family problems that create an environment of stress for the child. Unpredictability and inconsistency are typical in dysfunctional families. The alcoholic or emotionally unstable parent might be affectionate one moment and abusive the next, for no reason understandable to the child. An unhappy single mother might confide in her eldest child one hour, then push him or her into the background when her boyfriend arrives. An overwhelmed parent can easily volley between strict discipline one day, and complete oblivion to the child's behavior the next.

Children reared in such environments develop strong feelings of insecurity and confusion about reality. In order to find a sense of balance in their unstable environments, they may turn to dichotomous thinking. This gives them the illusion that they can predict reality more accurately. It also enables them to feel the security of boundaries in what is otherwise a chaotic world.

Such children often emerge into adulthood with a well-defined capacity to think in polar opposites. One set of behaviors is good, the opposite is bad. Life is black and white with little, if any, gray.

The concepts of "masculinity" and "femininity"

serve these adults well, particularly in their more rigid forms. They become guideposts, cues for behavior, when their sense of themselves as males or females is poorly defined. Raw from a wounded childhood, their personal insecurity often requires dichotomous thinking.

Thus men who are insecure in their male identity are often desperate to keep females relegated to definable roles and behaviors. By doing so they gain a sense of security. They can avoid anything characterized as "feminine." If he knows that women are defined by caring for babies, being secretaries and ironing altar cloths, the faltering male knows exactly what he has to avoid in order to "feel male." Keeping women locked into these roles becomes essential to his "masculinity." So does over-emphasizing "masculine" behaviors such as aggression and control in his own behavior. In this way he can be assured that he "looks male" to everyone else.

Studies have shown that people who come from dysfunctional backgrounds show more rigidity, more conservatism, more resistance to change and more opposition to the values of feminism than do individuals from stable backgrounds. The latter tend to be much more flexible in their thinking and behaving, and much less role bound. Gender security (being comfortable as a man if one is male, and comfortable as a woman if one is female) correlates highly with preferences for male-female equality and male-female role flexibility.

Moral Development or Male Development?

Jung was not the only psychological thinker who was influenced by patriarchy. Researchers and behavioral scientists of our day continue to fall victim to its assumptions. Several years ago, Lawrence Kohlberg attracted widespread attention for his pioneering work on the stages of moral development. Only after another researcher attempted to further study Kohlberg's newly identifed stages, did it come to light that all of Kohlberg's subjects had been male. He used 84 boys (no girls) and drew his conclusions on the moral stages of people based only on male experience. This is a good example of patriarchy in the 20th century. It is faithful to the patriarchal assumption: Male experience is normative; female experience derives from and can be measured against male experience.

When Kohlberg's categories were tested on females, they consistently fell short. The responses of women did not fit Kohlberg's categories. The women, as a group, placed much more emphasis on the relational consequences of moral decisions than they did on the objective rightness or wrongness of an action. The males in the original study had done just the opposite. Consequently, if one measured the moral development of women using Kohlberg's categories, it would have to be assumed that women, as a group, have a level of moral development that is deficient in comparison to males.

Other researches have also tended to identify male experience with human experience. They have concluded, in turn, that women who don't match male responses are less developed in the area under study. For example, Piaget looked to boys as the model for child development. When he observed differences in the way boys and girls used rules while playing games, he dismissed the girls' experience and reported that ". . . the legal sense . . . is far less developed in little girls than in boys" (Gilligan, p. 10).

Erikson followed a similar pattern. In charting the eight stages of psycho-social development, he noticed differences between males and females. For females, the stages of identity and intimacy are fused. Females tend to achieve a sense of identity in connection with forming relationships. For males, identity appears to be a separate process which precedes intimacy. Males seem less able to move into intimate relationships until they have a clear sense of identity. In spite of these differences, Erikson's model of psychosocial development virtually omits female experience, and identifies human development with male development. Erikson's eight stages of development list identity as preceding intimacy, even though this appears to be true only of males.

Virtually all influential researchers in human development have followed the same patriarchal pattern. Male experience becomes the norm. It also becomes that which is most valued.

The implications of ignoring female experience and female patterns are multiple. Expectations are established that are foreign to the inner experience of many women. This forces them to make a variety of uncomfortable and often confusing choices. They can ignore their experience and try to conform to the male norm. They can evaluate their relational preferences as somehow faulty or less noble and harbor a quiet sense of inferiority. Or they can feel judged according to a male standard and grow angry and alienated. Whatever adaptations they make to survive in a patriarchal world, the relational skills essential to partnership are less available to them, to society, and to the church.

One striking place where this has occurred is in women's religious communities. For years, Catholic nuns were cautioned against having "particular friendships." It was believed that close relationships would be detrimental to the development of a strong spiritual identity. This fear of intimacy may have arisen through the imposition of a male model of spirituality upon women's reality, an imposition women accepted for centuries. Warnings about "particular friendship" bear a striking similarity to Erikson's theory that a strong sense of identity must be achieved before one can engage in close relationships. Further, the reluctance to view intimacy as a companion of identity formation may have its roots more in patriarchy than in male reality. In actuality, the suspicion of interpersonal closeness has probably been as harmful to men as it has to women.

Neither Male Nor Female: Toward a Contemporary Understanding

Some fear that an emphasis on the similarities between males and females will eventually lead to a society of "droids"—people who have blended maleness and femaleness into a boring mass of sameness devoid of any distinction whatsoever. They picture women with crew-cuts, wearing black leather jackets and riding on motor-cycles with men who look just like them, down to their matching earrings. People with such a fear want male-female differences emphasized, or at least maintained. To them, a "feminine" woman and a "masculine" man, as defined by the stereotypes, represent the backbone of a stable society.

At the other extreme are those who resist all at-tempts on the part of social scientists to identify differ-ences between males and females. For this group, differ-ences undermine the ethic of equality. For these more radical feminists, there are no differences between males and females, other than the obvious anatomical ones that serve a purely procreative function. Hormones are the necessary support chemicals that produce second-ary sex characteristics that in turn enable procreation. They have no influence on behavior. Males are not in-nately more aggressive than females, they have simply been socialized to be so. Females are not more focused on relationships by nature, they have been taught to be this way by society. In this paradigm, masculinity and femi-ninity do not actually exist. They do not describe differ-ences that are real. They are only stereotypes that pro-duce the behavior they define.

Somewhere between these two extremes are those who hold a more moderate view of male-female differ-ences. They recognize that the masculine-feminine cate-gories of Jung fail to describe accurately many males and females in our society. They know that stereotypes can coerce behavior that does not fit with the natural preferences of some individuals. They have seen how po-larized male and female traits maintain sexist attitudes. At the same time, these people also believe that body chemicals, such as androgens and estrogens, may have a greater effect on human behavior than just reproductive readiness. They suspect that human genes may contain codes that influence male-female behavior as well as eye color.

In this perspective, part of the biblical call to be naked and without shame is a call to understand, as fully as possible, whatever differences and similarities there are. If Jung's trait theory is no longer adequate to describe psychological differences between women and men, this does not necessarily mean there are no differences. It simply means we need to take another, perhaps more scientific, look.

Those who stand at either extreme in the debate regarding male-female differences share at least one thing in common: whether they want to maintain the sexist stereotypes, or to call for radical obliteration of any differences other than the anatomical ones, they both fear nakedness. If there truly are no differences, the first group doesn't want to know it. If there are genuine differences yet to be discovered and understood, the second group doesn't want to see them. Naked and without shame. It has never been easy.

9
Beyond Patriarchy
Contemporary Developments in Male-Female Differences

In a recent Catholic weekly, Dolores Curran made the following distinction between males and females: "Men report facts. Women tell stories."

Throughout history, people have noticed differences that seem peculiar to the sexes. Those who observe these differences may not be scientists who gather and analyze objective data, but they are, nonetheless, keen observers of human interaction. It does not matter to them whether the variations they see have their roots in homes or hormones. What does matter is that people experience basic differences between the relational styles of males and females. These perceptions in turn have a significant impact on the interaction between women and men in our society.

By reason of their profession, behavioral scientists are interested in subjecting popular opinions to formal study. In the past, a major factor not taken into account in these studies was the patriarchal bias of the researchers. This bias has led to the development of theories about male-female differences that are now being called into question. We have already examined some of them.

Jung noticed that women focused more on relationships than did men, and he related this to women's particular need to belong. Erik Erikson noticed it too, but regarded it as insignificant. Jean Piaget observed it, and thought it was a deficit. Differences were interpreted with a patriarchal mindset—a bias that assumed male experience was the norm and women should be measured against it.

From Relational Deficits to Relational Potential

Is it a deficit to make decisions according to the consequences those choices will have for relationships, or is it a capacity for caring that society has failed to value? Is it some fragile need that compels women to seek attachment, or is it a potential for interpersonal relationships we have too long neglected? More importantly, if the claimed difference in relational emphasis between males and females constitutes a *true difference* between them, what causes it? Is there something in female genetics or body chemistry that causes this emphasis on relationships or are women socialized to care more about people?

Answers to these questions reflect the familiar nature-nurture debate that flourishes among behavioral scientists. Those who believe in the primacy of biology argue that males and females are bound to obey the dictates of their different hormones and genetically determined traits. Researchers who believe that the environment exerts more influence on behavior report that all of the observed differences in males and females, except the anatomical ones, are caused by the socialization process. Both sides can cite evidence for their varying positions.

Male-Female Differences: The Argument From Nature

Scientists know that the xy combination of the male genetic code causes the production of male hormones (androgens) early in fetal development. These hormones, they believe, are largely responsible for "male" characteristics like aggression, high activity level and competitiveness. Many studies have been done that demonstrate that certain behaviors, such as aggression, correlate with the level of androgens circulating in the blood. Similar studies have shown that male and female infants differ at birth in frequency of aggressive movements.

With regard to females, the xx combination produces estrogens which, in turn, determine "female" characteristics such as a desire to nurture, to focus on details, to express emotion and to show interest in communication. Studies have shown that female infants tend to focus their gaze on faces for longer periods of time than do male infants. Similar studies have demonstrated that crying is associated with higher levels of estrogen circulating in the blood.

Other researchers in this area have turned to evolution to study the causes of male-female differences. In ancient societies, they argue, women stayed together to care for children and keep the hearth, while men went in search of food. In order to transmit the traditions of the tribe to the young, and to maintain rapport among themselves, women needed to develop communication skills, and to be attentive to relational cues. Men, who often hunted alone or in small groups, had to keep silent as they waited for their prey or avoided danger in the wilds. They needed to be aggressive, to develop finely tuned spacial skills and precise movements. Over the centuries, females with the best relational abilities and males with the strongest sense of competition survived, and passed these characteristics on to their offspring. The evolutionary scientists theorize that male-female differences have evolved over the generations and are actually programmed into the genetic codes of women and men.

Male-Female Differences: The Argument From Nurture

The nurture scientists report that hospital attendants, parents and physicians treat male and female infants differently from birth. They tend to talk more to females, to speak gently and softly to them, and to cuddle them more. Male infants are directly addressed less frequently and in louder voices. They are also handled more roughly.

One group of researchers studied hospital visitors at a nursery. When the visitors thought the babies they were viewing were males, they "noticed" stereotypical masculine behavior. For example, when female new-borns were wrapped in blue blankets, viewers comments included: "Look at those fists. He's a little slugger!" When the same female infants were wrapped in pink blankets, viewers comments were much more apt to emphasize "those delicate little hands!" Male babies were greeted as "tigers" and noticed for their "good set of lungs" if they cried. Female babies were "little cuties" who had "such pretty blue eyes."

The nurture scientists argue that the differences we observe in males and females are programmed not by hormones and genes, but by the stereotypical ways we relate to children from the beginning. A female infant who is dressed in lace, looked upon as sweet and soft and handled with delicacy, will learn early in life to produce the behaviors that reflect her handling. A male child who is tossed in the air, dressed in a football jersey at two weeks, and regarded as a tough little guy, will likely oblige his parents with the "all boy" activity for which they yearn.

The Nature-Nurture Debate: What Does It Mean for Partnership?

The nature-nurture argument will no doubt be with us for a long time simply because we have much to understand about ourselves. We do not have all the answers. Human behavior is complex and defies easy attempts to explain its causes or predict its occurrence.

Whatever their causes, male and female differences do seem to extend well beyond anatomy. It is our belief that most, if not all, observable differences in women and men result from a complex and often inconsistent blend of innate biological factors and environmental learning. The chemicals and genetic codes of our bodies were fashioned by a loving God who designed all aspects of our humanity to function in integration. Our body chemistry does not stand in isolation from our behavior. Our genes are not cold computer programs that speak secretly to our anatomy, but have no message for our hearts. Rather, all aspects of our physiology are part of the sacred ground out of which we seek wholeness. At the same time, we are more than hormones encased in skin, robotic slaves to our genetic codes. In many ways, our external environments are partners to our bodies, fine tuning the complex interplay between drives and choices as we grow.

If scientific research in both the areas of nature and nurture can help us bring the inner environment of our bodies into greater harmony with the outer environment of our world, then humanity is one step closer to wholeness and God is served.

In the day to day world of relating, the causes of male-female differences seem to have less urgency than their effects. And yet, if the human community is going to grow toward partnership, we need to understand better what inhibits its development and enables its success. When we talk about partnership, we are talking about relationships. Partnership between women and men presupposes that both males and females have a desire and a capacity for forming relationships. Yet, popular observation and scientific research both assert that women are more relationally oriented than men. If they are correct, a serious problem exists for the partnership vision. More importantly, if they are correct and that is how God designed it, then the problem may be insurmountable.

We believe in a God who exists in a state of partnership and wrote the divine vision in our hearts. We do not believe that the God of partnership would tease us with a vision of equality and mutuality, and then design males and females with differing genetic and hormonal capacities for achieving it. If females are more relationally oriented than males, then we need to look, in the case of this particular difference, to our environments for clues. This is exactly what some researchers have done with regard to the apparent relational difference. Their findings are important in our quest for partnership.

Gender Identity and the Capacity for Partnership

One of the primary tasks of early childhood is the development of gender identity. In its earliest stage, this means that the young child must come to know whether it is male or female. The personal meaning of gender identity continues to change and evolve long past early childhood. But children usually understand their gender as a permanent condition by the age of three. This means that the male child comes to know that he is a boy, that he will always be a boy, and that being a boy is somehow different than being a girl. The female child learns that she is a girl, will always be a girl, and that girls and boys are different.

It is important not to confuse gender identity with sexual orientation. All children go though the process of coming to know that they are either boys or girls. The cognitive awareness or discovery of one's sexual orientation (homosexual, heterosexual, bisexual) is a different process and generally occurs later.

The development of the concept of gender identity happens around the time that the child first notices anatomical differences between males and females. Young children direct their earliest attention about gender differences to physical differences. Gradually, as they attempt to grasp the implications of the anatomical variations, they begin to make use of society's messages about maleness and femaleness. In a serious attempt to "fit in," they begin to model their behaviors after the women and men around them. As soon as a male child says to himself, "I am a boy," he must begin the task of coming to know what it means to be a boy. When the female child identifies herself as a girl, she undertakes the work of discovering the implications of her new self-definition. The concepts of maleness and femaleness that adults take for granted become monumental learning tasks of childhood, requiring intense observation, cognitive processing and energy expenditure.

In addition to assimilating the raw data about male and female anatomy, the child must also begin to develop a sense of ownership of his or her gender. Each child begins early to prepare for the day when he or she will reach out to another and say, "This at last is bone of my bones and flesh of my flesh . . ." (Gn 2:23). Before that day comes, the child must know and value its own flesh. Before the advent of adulthood, it must be able to stand before its own nakedness without shame. The process of gender identity formation, then, begins as a surface journey into the newly discovered and exciting world of genital differences. As it continues, it carries its young travelers into the deeper world of the meaning those differences have, and the commitment they will require. The gender identity journey begins with the child's cognitive discovery of flesh and culminates when the adult has entered his or her flesh, experienced it as very good and felt the desire to share it.

The child's social environment plays a key role in helping or hindering the process of gender identity formation. Historically, both church and society have encouraged women to take primary responsibility for child rearing. At least until the recent emphasis on shared parenting, women have obliged. In this culture, the earliest social environment for children is predominantly female. Approximately 80 percent of American children spend 80 percent of their waking time in the care of females—mothers, day care workers and baby sitters. This means that children, whether male or female, must come to a sense of gender identity in a largely female environment. Consequently, something different is required of the child, depending on whether that child is a little boy or a little girl.

As female children come to learn that they are girls, they usually become aware of what this means for them from *within* their environment. To know "girlness," they study, mimic and spend time around the women who are, for the most part, a constant in their environments. They can look at their mothers, baby sitters or day care workers and say to themselves: "I am a girl. She is a girl. We are alike!" Female children tend to stay near their female caretakers and attach to them in order to gradually come to know what it means to be a girl.

In contrast, in order to come to an awareness of what it means to be a boy, the male child must leave his largely female environment. As he looks around, he must say to himself: "I am a boy. She (caretaker) is not a boy. We are different." The male child must then separate from the environment that usually does not offer him consistent daytime models for his budding maleness. If he stays too close to it, he cannot discover "boyness." He must move away from femaleness in search of maleness.

This contrast in the journey little boys and girls make to achieve gender identity, forges early patterns that persist long into adulthood. For each of them, a way of relating is being learned. Girls learn to draw close. They become adept at focusing on a significant other. They experience connection. They learn to associate a sense of self-identity with being in relationship. The security of the relationship will help determine the security of their gender identity. Later, in adulthood, the experience that will feel most threatening to them is the absence of important relationships in their lives.

Boys, on the other hand, learn to pull away. They turn their focus to the outside world. They experience separation. They learn to associate personal well-being with being "on their own." To the extent that they feel secure in their quest, they will experience a connection between strong gender identity and independence. As adults, they will tend to be most threatened by a loss of this independence. For many males, the closer they perceive a relationship to be, the greater is their need to pull back and re-establish a sense of separateness.

Relationships or Rules: The Play of Boys and Girls

Studies of the play of boys and girls bear this out. Little boys leave the house earlier, go farther and stay away longer than little girls do. While this tendency has been observed for some time, it has usually been interpreted with a male bias, namely, that boys are more courageous than girls, who seem to prefer the security of play indoors. Current research, however, may indicate something of the opposite.

The competitive games preferred by boys may well represent a primordial need to "win" separation from the women who carried them, nursed them and surrounded them with their female essence during their earliest years. As part of achieving their male identity, little boys must begin to play on a different team, fight the other side, and seek victory over the female forces that have, up until now, enveloped their lives. Part of the often documented male need to "prove himself" may well have its roots in the little boy's need to "prove" that he is not female—that his connection to female figures during gestation, infancy and early childhood does not make a statement about his gender. Competing with opposite forces through games and wars may be one of the ways males enact their separation from women.

Playground studies show that boys prefer games where there are winners and losers. The framework that holds these games together are rules and boundaries. Obedience to the rules and adherence to the boundaries are a prerequisite for staying in the game. To resolve a dispute, young boys may even appeal to an authority figure like a parent or an older sibling. His decisions might be disliked, or questioned, but they are usually obeyed. When boys have a disagreement, it is common for a fight to break out. But soon, the rules are appealed to and everyone goes back to the game.

Unless they are being coached by competition oriented teachers or parents, little girls seem to prefer turntaking and role-playing games, such as hopscotch and "house." Rules and boundaries play a minor role in their games, and tend to be much more flexible, often evolving and changing as the game progresses. In a recent study involving second grade girls during recess, the following behavior was observed: Six or seven little girls were playing hopscotch. (Note that in most games preferred by little girls, there is no exact number of players.) During the game, one little girl jumped into a square, landing with one foot on the chalk line. Two or three others told her she had to go back to the starting line. She objected and an argument began. Within minutes, another little girl pulled out the chalk and re-drew the hopscotch line, demonstrating that her friend needed a bigger square in which to put her foot. All players studied the new line, agreed that it was better and went on with the game.

This is an example of what Piaget described as a less developed "legal sense" characteristic of girls. While it seems to be true that girls do not give rules an unbending place of honor in their games, identifying this as a lack of development is an example of applying patriarchal mentality to female experience. It is saying that male experience is normal, and that females should do what males do or be judged as deficient. Using feminist consciousness, we would say that little girls place greater value on compromise than on rigid obedience to rules. For them, the outcome of relationships is more important than compliance to regulations that have no particular importance in themselves.

Those who have taken the time to watch children play come to some of the same conclusions as do the research scientists. Boys games revolve around rules. When the rules are violated, an authority figure may be called in to settle the dispute. After being reminded of the rules, or punished for a violation of them, boys generally go back to the game. Eventually, someone wins and someone loses. The winners celebrate their victory and the losers resolve to practice more and try harder next time. For boys, *winning* becomes the primary value. Getting a bloody nose, shouting at the opponent and relishing the win is all part of the game.

With little girls, different behaviors emerge. Games

revolve not around rules but around relationships and taking turns. Rules change and evolve to fit the situation. Girls tend not to like it when someone feels bad, hence games involving losers are minimized. When girls have disputes during play, they tend to get another turn (a second chance), to change the rules or to quit the game. Little girls' games rarely appeal to outside authority figures for a final decision. For girls, the primary value is *relating*. It involves trying on someone else's clothes or make-up, inventing dialogue and working out the rules so that everyone can stay connected.

The Significance of Play Differences of Boys and Girls

Are the differences observed between the games and play of little boys and girls merely interesting but inconsequential to later behavior, or do the differences manifest themselves in adult interaction?

Some researchers suggest that early childhood play teaches behaviors that forge the patterns of adult interactions. Children who divide into teams of winners and losers and compete with each other, for whatever reason, grow up being comfortable in a world divided into allies and opponents, winners and losers. They are familiar with the feelings of competitiveness.

On the other hand, children who grow up playing house and taking on the roles of different family members learn to identify with the experience of others. They learn empathy skills. They grow up knowing what it feels like to crawl into someone else's skin. The world is a family, often an idealized one, where everyone talks to everyone else.

Do little boys who divide themselves into opposing teams and compete with each other take their experience with them when they grow up? Do they become the males who run the world and see life in competitive terms? Does the "winner vs. loser" style of their youthful activities show itself in their grown up ways of relating to those who oppose them? Does a mentality that says the rules of the game are more important than the feelings of the people express itself in the larger world of social institutions and corporate bureaucracies? Does maintaining the competitive edge replace the human need to maintain relationships?

If we answer "yes" to these questions, even more urgent questions must be raised. Should the particular style of one of the sexes have dominance in the way the world is run? Is it healthy to look only to males for leadership and authority in the church? Or, like the ancient people of Bora Bora, have we forgotten something vital? Have we left behind something significant to our journey? Have we lost sight of the vision of partnership?

These questions are not an attempt to negate male experience. Nor is it an effort to suggest that female experience is superior. Our purpose is not to continue to polarize the sexes but rather to end that polarization. In so doing, we must name our present world and church reality. Patriarchy is the ideology that consistently pervades our political, educational, social and religious systems. Male models of governance, learning, relating and believing have dominated most aspects of human experience. The balance that ought to exist between male-female approaches has been lost. Consequently, the dimensions of male experience that are in themselves good and necessary to humanity no longer have a sense of containment.

The faulty principle that says "if a little is good, more is better" is as unhealthy here as it is when applied to food. Whenever one perspective dominates the human community, something essential is lost. When the enforcement of rules is not tempered by compassion, the central value of Christianity is abandoned. When competition loses the capacity to compromise, wars break out. When the quest for independence results in an inability to be vulnerable, intimacy cannot take place. All around us, there is too much war, and too little intimacy.

When women are critical of male dominance, their concerns can be misunderstood as a rejection of male experience, or of men in general. What is really at stake is not criticism of healthy male preferences, but rather, criticism of male preferences taken to the extreme, even for men.

Because male dominance is so pervasive in our world and church, and female influence is subsequently diminished, re-winning a sense of biblical partnership may require some temporary over-emphasis on what has been missing. We can also expect to see further criticism of male styles of influence. However, it is important to keep both the over-emphasis and the criticism in perspective. The one is being over-emphasized because, like the widow's coin, it has been lost and must be found. The other is being criticized because it has over-stepped its boundaries, lost sight of its limitations and consequently distorted its own goodness. In the long run, however, the goal of partnership is to move beyond the alienation of the fall to a place where balance is restored. There, both males and females can experience shared dignity and mutual delight in their differing gifts.

Ultimately, partnership calls for respect for rules, balanced with the capacity to bend them when compassion demands it. It welcomes a kind of playful competition that does not hurt or oppress people; a competition that has not forgotten sensitivity and caring. It values healthy independence, an independence as eager for relationships as it is able to stand alone.

Relational Differences and Their Implications for Ministry

Since males generally place greater value on competition, independence and obedience to rules; and females give more importance to compromise, cooperation and loyalty to relationships, we can understand why women and men will experience tension when they minister together.

In recent years in the Catholic community, we have seen these different styles of male-female relating come into direct conflict. Often, the conflict has been between members of women's religious congregations and leaders of the institutional church. Frequently, the women are asking for compassion, dialogue and openness. They are willing to travel to Rome and to engage in face-to-face conversation with those in leadership positions. They want to discuss tensions, to face problems directly and to have involvement in shaping the decisions that affect their lives.

Too often they have encountered disappointment in their efforts. Church leaders have viewed their requests not as invitations to share values and reach agreements about areas of conflict, but rather, as intrusions into their domain of leadership. Authorities have refused to dialogue about differences and have demanded obedience to the rules. Where the women saw an opportunity for compromise and a need to talk, church leaders often perceived a competitive challenge to their authority and a need to win. Where the women sought relationships, the men opted for separation.

Some of the recent interactions between women in religious congregations and Vatican authorities reveal a curious resemblance to the patterns seen in the games of early childhood. In some ways, the women are redrawing the chalk line. In contrast, male authorities quote the rules that have to be obeyed by anyone who wants to stay in the game. The tensions with Rome may reflect one of the areas where male dominance has become skewed; where rules seem more important than relationships, where vulnerability has given way to insulation and where winning takes precedence over compromise. Unfortunately, many women in the church today are weary of what often seems like a game. They would rather quit.

Does the style of leadership that refuses dialogue and demands obedience to its rules reflect the values and vision of the gospel, or is it more reminiscent of a style of relating that flows from patriarchy? Does it point to the vision of partnership, or to the upbringing characteristic of the patriarchal family?

In the patriarchal family, caring for children is the special role of women. In such a family, little boys grow up needing to separate from women, to lean on rules and to experience competition. As long as the institutional church continues to stress patriarchal models of family, we will continue to see a leadership style in the church that flows from the behaviors learned in childhood. We will also continue to see tensions in marriage and in ministry that do not need to be there. Perhaps one of the most significant things the institutional church can do for partnership is to intensify its emphasis on the importance of both mothers and fathers being intimately involved in the care and nurturing of children.

We do not yet know what kind of impact this will have on children, but the early signs are positive. When fathers, or male caretakers, provide a consistent presence for children, are actively involved in their care from birth and offer them models of warmth, we can expect the relational skills of their children to be enhanced. Little boys, particularly, will do more attaching, thus enabling them to grow up with greater capacities to form relationships. We will still very likely see a greater degree of separating with boys than with girls, simply because boys, as they work out their male gender identity, will continue to need to move away from the natural connection they have with the women who gave them birth. But this need to separate will stand alongside a familiarity with attachment.

The High Cost of Patriarchy

In a patriarchal system, males are taught to be self-sufficient, tough and invincible, almost from birth. They are encouraged to hide their feelings, particularly their more tender ones, and to be strong, or at least look strong, at all times. They learn early in life that crying is sissy, and being gentle is cowardice. By the time they are teen-agers, many learn that being attracted to someone requires the behaviors of conquest. The ideal of independence and the practice of macho behaviors are made for each other. Even males who do not adhere to this patriarchal system are often reluctant to be vulnerable or engage in the kind of healthy openness that says in attitude or in words: I am afraid. I need you. Stay awake with me, just for a little while.

Women, on the other hand, are usually given the opposite message. It is imperative that they not look too self-sufficient, lest men be threatened by them. The dependency ideal requires that they lean on others, seek advice from men and show just enough emotional transparency to attract protectors. Confiding in close friends and sharing secrets is all part of the mystique that keeps women from the extreme independence that will make them "masculine."

While we often want to believe that these opposites attract, what transpires all too frequently is that too much "opposite" prevents real partnership from taking place. What is defined as independence by the male is often experienced as a lack of caring by the female. What she describes as communicating, he can feel as invading. These differences can cause males to retreat into self-protective isolation, and females to become overly involved in re-establishing the connection between them. When one person in a relationship is emotionally aloof, and the other is emotionally preoccupied, there is not much common ground for real intimacy. Under these circumstances, marriages falter, ministry suffers and male church leaders become even more disconnected from those whom they are trying to lead.

For men, the claim to dominance has been costly in terms of developing intimacy skills. When one must carry the full weight of economic responsibility and leadership for family, church or world, there is seldom a safe time to let defenses down and feel needy, to lean on someone else for awhile or even to cry. Interior tenderness cannot develop out of a perpetual exterior of tough control. This means the loss of a critical component of intimacy. Being a winner in the office, being awarded the bishop's ring or the cardinal's red hat, too often means paying the price the fall demands: hiding needs, avoiding vulnerability, living with emotional isolation—the very existence God did not want for the earth creature.

For women, settling into a subordinate role has usually meant trading self-esteem for superficial security. It has demanded that women blunt their awareness of discrimination or oppression in society or church. For some women, practicing the patriarchal virtues of self-denial and docility brought them dangerously close to masochistic self-annihilation. For all women, the price of patriarchy has been reduced religious and political influence, an uphill struggle to develop natural leadership skills and a pervasive demeaning of genuine feminine gifts. As sisters of Eve, they carry the blame and guilt of the fall. They bear their children in pain and often raise them alone. Their men lord it over them. Their sons rise up and kill each other. It is not what the God who fashioned *ezer k negdo* had in mind.

This One at Last

Re-winning the vision of partnership demands that we live by *its* values, and not the values of the fall. We need to give up the behaviors that perpetuate the fall— the blaming, the hiding, the diminishing, the shaming. We need to condemn patriarchy as the antithesis of partnership, and abandon the practices that flow from it; practices that continue to polarize women and men. The vision of partnership invites us to share power, to welcome mutual vulnerability and to embrace our nakedness without shame. It urges us to see our sisters and brothers as bone of our bone and flesh of our flesh.

Authentic partnership is not brought about by a ministerial "equal opportunity act" whereby proportionate numbers of women and men serve as lectors, musicians, parish council members or even curial decision making bodies. Partnership does not result from gender assignment. It results from the hard work of communication among women and men. Partnership begins its slow growth when women and men internalize the stance of the first biblical partners: the willingness to be naked, radically naked psychologically, emotionally and spiritually. It can only happen when women and men strip themselves of masks of self-sufficiency and abandon feeble attempts to hide their vulnerabilities from one another. Such partnership rests solidly on the belief that such nakedness is central to God's creative intention.

Partnership is an experience of inner connection brought about by a consistent commitment to the demanding, painful and sometimes messy work of human relating. It implies the willingness to listen without judging; the ability to say clearly and honestly what one thinks, feels and believes; the capacity to experience compassion; and a finely tuned awareness of one's behavioral style and inner motivation. It requires the courage to name conflicts and tensions before they become divisions, and a desire to maintain interpersonal bonds that surpasses the desire to maintain control.

When genuine partnership exists, what does it look like? What do we see?

We see a condition in which God's sons do not experience their maleness as a springboard to power, or where God's daughters do not experience their femaleness as an obstacle to it. Rather, both have equal access to leadership and decision making at home, in society and in the church—an access limited only by individual differences in interest, ability or needs in the community.

We see a condition in which personality characteristics such as tenderness, strength, nurturance, assertiveness, gentleness, emotional expressiveness and cognitive ability are not divided into ''masculine'' and ''feminine'' categories but are regarded as human and witnessed by any person taking his or her baptism seriously.

We see a condition where the proven ability to live the partnership vision is more important in the selection of church leaders and sacramental ministers than is the presence of male genitalia.

We see a condition where pastors are known less for their hard nosed fidelity to church disciplines and rules, and more for their fidelity to compassion.

Whether in homes, in rectories, in convents, in chancery offices or in Rome, we see self-protection giving way to self-disclosure, secrecy giving way to openness and misunderstandings giving way to dialogue.

Where partnership exists, we see reverence toward one another's maleness and femaleness spilling over into reverence for the earth, the soil and water, the air and the forests, the animals and fishes and all of God's children with their multi-colored skins.

Only from the stance of partnership taken dead seriously can the church dare to speak against the many oppressions riveting our universe.

The path to partnership is a shared journey. Humanity, in its infancy, began in mutuality. Women and men can only grow toward wholeness as *individuals* if they do it *in partnership*. So implicated are women and men in each other's journey toward completion that the oppression of one implies the oppression, in some way, of the other. If the process of growth of one of them stops, the other is also crippled. When women experience a stunted sense of dignity as female persons, something is stunted in men as well. In both Genesis accounts, as one of them is shaped, the other emerges. This is the trajectory of God's creativity. *Ezer k negdo* is not a remote Hebrew phrase that describes a past theological event. It is a call in the present moment enfleshed in the depth of every woman and man. It is a call that seeks mutuality. It aches for partnership. It yearns to hear again the primordial words that echo deep in our being: This one at last!

10
Reverence in Relationships
Sexuality and Partnership

The Sexual Revolution

"The Revolution Is Over!" In the spring of 1984 this announcement appeared in banner headlines on the cover of *Time* magazine. The editors were referring specifically to the sexual revolution and its cultural implications for the United States. According to *Time*, this cultural revolution is finished.

Few people would question that there has been a transformation of our understanding and experience of sexuality during the past quarter-century (cf. Nelson, *Christian Century,* pp. 187 ff.). Several factors have contributed to this upheaval. Some of them were related to the interpersonal aspects of sexuality: a more permissive attitude toward sex outside of marriage, teen-age pregnancies, soaring divorce rates, single-parent families and the explicit portrayal of sexual topics in the media. Other factors had to do with the "politics of sex"— the changing roles of women in the work place and in society, new forms of birth control and reproductive technology and the emergence of issues surrounding homosexuality.

The permissive attitudes of the last few decades have borne painful results in the form of alienated lives and personal brokenness. There is a widespread sense of disillusionment with casual sexual affairs and one-night stands. Promiscuity is being replaced by responsibility, a new emphasis on fidelity in relationships and an attempt to re-win traditional family values. The earlier appearance of herpes, and more recently the epidemic of AIDS, have begun to bring about an ethic of "safe sex," if not of responsible sex.

Does this mean that the sexual revolution is over? While it may be true that a more careful approach to sexual sharing is replacing the permissive attitudes of the recent past, it is by no means clear that the task of transformation has been accomplished. If anything, on the deeper level of human values, the revolution may be just getting under way. The search to understand human intimacy and its implications is only in its initial stages. The significance of covenantal relationships in marriage and other forms of friendship are waiting to be creatively explored and lived. The relationship of human sexuality and Christian values needs development and further clarification. In short, the real revolution—the revolution of human partnership—is just beginning.

Sexuality and Partnership

In the earlier chapters we addressed the biblical and historical background of partnership ministry. We also examined the challenges that face the contemporary church in continuing to implement the collegial approach to pastoral leadership. But the issue of collaboration between women and men cannot be limited to a discussion of leadership styles and communication skills. Eventually the question of maleness and femaleness must become part of the discussion. Beyond that we must also face the deeper issues of sexuality and its role in ministerial partnership.

Unfortunately, there is a tendency both in our culture and in the church to reduce sexuality to biology, specifically to genital expressiveness and the questions that surround it. In the reflections that follow, we are speaking of sexuality in a much broader context. Sexuality, in its deepest roots, is the other-orienting energy of human life that makes all relationships possible, whether or not they are expressed in a genital manner. "Male and female God created them," the author of Genesis tells us, "in the image of the divine, God created them" (Gn 1:27). The Hebrew author is implying that it is precisely in our sexual reality—in our embodiment as woman and man—that we image the divine. Because our sexuality is such a permeating and constitutive dimension of our humanity, it affects everything we are and do. Every relationship has a sexual aspect, since we relate to one another as males and females.

In this chapter we will explore sexuality as it relates to partnership ministry in the contemporary church. It is a vital aspect of understanding how women and men can be more effective ministers on behalf of the gospel.

Sexuality and Religion

Let us look first at the wide screen of history and the development of human consciousness. From the earliest dawning of human awareness there has been a dynamic interrelationship between sexuality and religious experience. Sometimes this relationship is fruitful and generative; at other times it is alienating and tension-filled. The encounter with the holy and the power of our embodied energy are part of our daily experience, even when we do not recognize or name them as explicitly religious or sexual. Our daily experiences of incarnation transcend our comprehension and ability to articulate their meaning; they move us into mystery. We cannot reduce sexuality or religion to scientific information or a collection of data; they envelop us and ground us in an experience larger than ourselves. They express in us a rootedness with our genetic and evolutionary past, while at the same time calling us to live in relationship in the present.

The French philosopher and theologian Paul Ricoeur speaks of three major eras in the relationship between sexuality and religion. Examining these stages of development can serve as framework for the more immediate question of sexuality and partnership in our time.

Identification. Historically, the earliest relationship between sexuality and religion was that of a profound attunement. In fact, at this stage of evolution we can describe it as an absence of differentiation, perhaps even an absorption of one into the other. This is the era of goddess worship and female images of the holy. We see evidence of this identification of religion and sexuality in the sacred symbols, the form and content of worship and the meaning ancient peoples attached to sexual experience. The divine energy is located not in a transcendent world but in the cosmos itself, especially in the reproductive powers of the earth and of human life. Flowing from this sense of divine immanence is an instinctive awe and reverence for the cycles of the seasons and the rhythms life and fertility. Goddess worship involved ceremonies that "sacramentalized" the cosmic energy of life in ritual sexual relationships. Sexual union is a participation in the sacred rhythm of life; to reproduce is to share directly in the power of divinity.

Separation. With the further evolution of culture, a significant differentiation began to take place between religion and sexuality. Male gods began to replace the worship of the goddess; patriarchal patterns began to dominate cultural and family life; rational forms of thought challenged the participative power of myth and sacred rite.

In its initial stages this shift manifested itself in a primordial fear and anxiety men had toward women's mysteries. This apprehension eventually moved beyond a cultural suspicion to become an outright oppression of women and their place in society.

This period of history roughly parallels the emergence of the world's great religions. During these centuries a more rationalist way of thinking developed that demythologized the former meanings of the cosmos and sexuality. Reality came to be understood as a hierarchical "ladder of being," with men envisioned as higher on the scale of creation than women. The sacred became limited to the transcendent, the untouchable, the spiritual. Women were viewed as embodying the more earthy, sensuous and procreative roles in life. In place of the earlier role of myth and the fertility rites a dualistic understanding of religion and life gradually developed. Sexuality was often viewed as a distraction to the life of mind and spirit; it became limited to a small part of cosmic order, namely that of procreation within the institution of marriage. The power of sexuality was to be restrained by the discipline of mind over matter, spirit over flesh.

During this period of human history the differentiation of religion and sexuality sometimes went to extremes. The dualistic thinking of movements such as Gnosticism and Manicheism articulated a deep felt alienation between sexuality and religious experience. Evil became identified with matter and the flesh, whereas the soul and the world of spirit were thought of as the pathway to the good.

Integration. We have now entered a third period in our religious-sexual development. Today we are faced with the challenge of reuniting the sacred and the sexual in human experience. It is no longer possible to view sexuality as a distraction to the life of mind and spirit. The sexual dimension of our lives permeates our entire being; it reaches to the center of our personhood and needs to be reverenced as a source of spiritual energy. We are realizing today that sexuality and spirituality are not enemies but friends.

This movement toward integration is taking place only with great difficulty. At this stage it is a countercultural movement with strong biblical roots and a holistic vision of human relationships. It is unfolding in a culture marked by the breakdown of family values and fears surrounding the meaning of sexuality. On the one hand the evidence of sexual exploitation in our culture appears to be even more widespread than ever before. On the other hand, there has been a strong reaction against patriarchal oppression with its sexist attitudes and its devaluation of the earth and bodiliness. A renewed interest in myth and the desire to recover the vision of goddess worship often accompanies this quest of the human spirit.

But this movement is more than an attempt to recover the ancient past; it is not just a question of returning to an undifferentiated sense of unity between sexuality and religion. The challenge of this stage of human development is to integrate the primordial unity and immediacy of the first period with the self-consciousness and spiritual values of the second. A holistic spirituality is emerging that celebrates our unity with our bodies, with one another and with all of creation. In the lives of many quiet prophets—the visionary women and men of our age—we can begin to trace this shift from alienation toward integration. It is as though we are living on the fault-line of human history, poised between fear and anticipation, as we watch the patterns of relationships and the new configurations of love begin to take shape around us.

The Challenge of Our Age

We have arrived, in the words of the U.S. Bishops, at a "new moment" in human evolution. In our time, history is not just the flow of events that happens to us. It is rather the task we share, both communally and individually, to *shape* the direction of human events on this planet. This sense of responsibility is applicable not only to the actual decisions and policies we make as a human community; more fundamentally it refers to the values and visions that are the motivation and framework for our decisions.

What are these values? What vision will make claim on humanity's imagination as we begin the third millennium of Christian history? Specifically, what vision of human sexuality and partnership will guide our decisions and policies surrounding collaboration? What set of values will determine how women and men relate together in public service and in Christian ministry? What is the underlying vision of relationality that will shape our experience of friendship, love and intimacy? How can Christianity nurture and give direction to this "third era" in the development of human sexuality? How can the church as a community of believers take a leadership role in the challenge to integrate sexuality and religious experience?

These are the questions we want to explore in the remainder of this chapter. Beneath the issue of women's role in the church is the deeper issue of sexuality and power. Beyond the discussion of collaborative ministry there lies this more insistent challenge to the church and its mission. This challenge will not disappear or go away because of our unwillingness to face it. It cannot be ignored without disastrous consequences. Put simply, it is the challenge of re-imaging the meaning and context of sexuality.

Basic Human Needs

As a step toward re-imaging the meaning of sexuality and human relationships, let us explore briefly the fundamental hungers of our hearts—those basic needs that are a precondition for growth toward wholeness and holiness.

Physical Security. In order for human beings to flourish and grow, they must have the basic necessities to sustain life: food, shelter, clothing and the other fundamental means of survival. These life-sustaining necessities must be available on a reasonably secure and perduring basis if health and development are to be maintained.

Personal Relationships. It is obvious that we are social creatures. Human persons are not able to achieve maturity and integration without a community setting. We cannot become whole without interpersonal relationships and some degree of intimacy in our lives.

Affirmation/Self-Esteem. The third basic need is related to the awareness of our dignity and worth as persons. In order to be motivated for further development, each of us needs some basic experience of affirmation and recognition. We need to know, in other words, that we matter, that our lives and our presence make a difference to someone.

Sin: *The Brokenness of Life*

When these three fundamental hungers of the human heart are met, we can release the creative energies within us. We discover that we can grow toward wholeness of life. But what happens if these basic needs become distorted or somehow turned aside from their true goal? What effect will this have on our relationships and the quality of our lives? How will this deviancy affect our development?

We can answer these questions from a number of perspectives. On the experiential level, we have learned a great deal about distorted human needs from the treatment of addictive behaviors. In one sense an addiction is simply the pursuit of a basic need in such an exaggerated, unbalanced manner that our lives literally become "out of control." Psychologically, we can describe this condition as dysfunctional or emotionally destructive. In the perspective of Christian morality it is called *sin*. We are not just speaking here of individual acts that might violate an ethical law, but of an interior stance of the heart that is distorted, compulsive and sometimes even violent.

In an introduction to a recent Spanish translation of the New Testament, liberation theologian Juan Mateos describes these inward stances of brokenness as *claiming, controlling* and *climbing*. He sees them as the ways in which human sinfulness manifests itself both individually and in the social structures of oppression. They represent the demonic, broken dimensions of human life, often clothing themselves in the guise of social respectability. The evangelists portray Jesus as struggling with and overcoming the attitudes of claiming, controlling and climbing through his temptations in the wilderness. In his public ministry Jesus escalates this struggle with darkness; he names the demonic stances as they disclose themselves in the social and religious structures of his age. He confronts the oppression and exploitation that is taking place in human relationships; he touches the raw nerve of racism, sexism, elitism and hypocrisy; he speaks the truth in a manipulative and posturing world. In the end, this commitment to truth and compassion brings about Jesus' suffering and death.

The resurrection of Jesus conquered death and evil, but it did not end the confrontation with sin and brokenness; that struggle continues to unfold in our lives and relationships. It is important to "name the demons" as they appear in our hearts and social structures today.

Claiming is a radical distortion of our need for physical security and well-being. It is the attitude that proclaims: "This is mine, not yours; and I want more of it!" It is the perennial temptation to turn the kingdom into a "thingdom"—the illusory world of possessions, collectibles and luxury items. Claiming is consumerism out of control, a nightmare of insider trading, white collar crime and greed clothed in the language of the American dream.

Controlling is a destructive, manipulative stance toward human relationships. It turns the I-Thou of love and compassion into the I-It of competition and rivalry. Controlling assumes that dominative power is the primary social energy—not power *with* or power *for*, but power *over*; not the authentic energy of community, but the dominative force of manipulation. On a personal level controlling can manifest itself in everything from the silent treatment to physical or sexual abuse; on the level of social systems it often appears as racism, elitism or sexism.

Climbing is a twisted preoccupation with fame, the unbridled search for public recognition based on illusory accomplishments or notoriety. It is the temptation to think of our worth in terms of our public profile or our accomplishments rather than in the quality of our lives and our commitments. Our culture, with its emphasis on personalities and personas, only serves to reinforce this illusion.

From Paranoia to Metanoia

Claiming, controlling, climbing: In contemporary terms we might describe these attitudes as the "consumer trip," the "power trip," and the "ego trip." No matter what words we use to describe them, however, these destructive stances are ultimately forms of denial and escape. They are, in the fundamental meaning of the term, "paranoid"—illusory, frightened approaches to life. They are ways of running away from our humanity and our vulnerability to one another. They are posturings in an unreal world, a form of flight from God.

The evangelists not only describe the ways in which Jesus confronted these broken stances toward life; they also outline the alternative way of living that ought to replace them—the fullness of life Jesus promises those who are willing to follow him. Jesus invites humanity to experience the most radical of all transformations—the journey of conversion, which leads from *paranoia* to *metanoia,* from illusion to truth, from isolation to authentic community.

In the Christian tradition we have given names to these transformed attitudes of the heart. If claiming, controlling and climbing are indicative of "paranoid" or sinful behavior, then we can say that *poverty, chastity* and *obedience* are characteristic of a "metanoid" or a converted way of life.

Evangelical Counsels or Gospel Mandates?

For centuries we have referred to these three virtues or habits of life as the "evangelical counsels." In its original context, this designation pointed to a freely chosen life of "perfection," which was above and beyond the commitment required of an ordinary disciple. Unfortunately, this leaves us with the impression that although poverty, chastity and obedience are certainly worthwhile charisms, they are not necessarily intrinsic to every Christian's baptismal commitment.

In the context in which we are speaking here, however, it seems important to expand the significance of the evangelical counsels by rooting them more deeply in the gospel itself. When poverty, chastity and obedience are placed in the wider setting of Jesus' teaching, especially the Sermon on the Mount and the parables regarding the kingdom, we are faced with an inescapable conclusion. They can no longer be considered evangelical *counsels*; rather they must be approached as gospel *mandates* for all Christians.

This in turn leads us to another difficulty—one that has to do with the practical significance of these three virtues. The words themselves have a long and venerable tradition in Christian history, but their meaning has become obscure and even confusing for many believers. There may be a value in retaining the terms, but we must at least strive to redefine their significance.

It is awkward, for example, to speak of poverty as a virtue, when in many parts of the world it is experienced as a paralyzing and debilitating evil for millions of people. Over the last decades the United States has waged several "wars on poverty," most of which left destitution still in control. Poverty only becomes virtuous when we have enough of the necessities of life that we can freely choose to limit our consumption of the world's goods. In reality, therefore, we are speaking of *simplicity in life-style* —the responsibility all Christians have to conserve and share the earth's natural resources. "We must learn to live simply," writes Elizabeth Seton, "in order that others may simply live." Simplicity in lifestyle is the opposite of an attitude of claiming.

The same re-visioning needs to take place when we speak of obedience. While it is clear that children need to obey the loving guidance of their parents, the familial metaphor of submission does not seem appropriate when applied to a community of adults. As we have seen earlier, the language of the patriarchal family, when applied to religious congregations or parish communities, has severe limitations. The Christian vocation is ultimately a call to adult commitment. This act of free, self-conscious choice excludes the usual understanding of "blind" obedience. Obedience is not the act of giving over our responsibility to someone else; rather it is the choice to *be responsible* to the needs and mission of the wider community. The root meaning of obedience is to *listen*, that is, to shift our attention beyond our isolated selves to the relational bonds that unite us to others. Obedience as a gospel mandate is therefore related to *responsible listening in community*. It is the opposite of an attitude of climbing.

Chastity: Loving Reverence in Relationships

There is a strong need in today's church and society to develop a more positive meaning for chastity. The popular understanding of this virtue is, for the most part, negative and lifeless; it usually focuses on the absence of unlawful sexual expression in relationships. Thus the parameters with which we understand the meaning of chastity are primarily biological and physical rather than personal and relational.

In the context of the gospel message this understanding of chastity is far too limiting and confining. As we are approaching it here, chastity is not, in the first place, concerned with what one does or does not do with one's genitals. Rather it has to do with the *fundamental stance of our hearts* toward our brothers and sisters. Obviously this basic attitude in relationships also has implications regarding the ways we express our affection and our sexual feelings, but its primary focus is relational, not genital.

Perhaps we can gain an important clue to this deeper meaning of chastity by exploring its opposing attitude. As we have seen, poverty is a way of living that overcomes claiming; obedience is a habit of the heart that transcends climbing. The opposite of chastity is the attitude of *controlling*. The real sin of unchastity is not that it is physical or sexual, but that it is exploitive and manipulating. Chastity is a way of living that overcomes our tendencies to control other people, whether that domination is physical, emotional or specifically sexual. In short, chastity is *loving reverence in relationships*. It is a powerful and transforming way of living in community, the practical and daily enfleshment of *agape*. Chastity is not an ascetical choice by an elite group in the church to forego genital, sexual expressiveness; it is a gospel mandate for all Christians. It must be an integral dimension of every disciple's behavior, whether one is celibate, single, vowed religious or married.

In our catechesis and sacramental formation, we have not focused on this deeper, gospel meaning of a chaste life. The result has been an ambiguity, even a confusion about the way we understand relationships and human sexuality. The confusion flows from a residual Gnosticism that tends to condemn sexuality itself instead of confronting the real sin of controlling, exploitive behavior. Thus there is the classic double message engaged couples may receive from the church: "Sex is dirty; save it for someone you love." What we really want to communicate is a far different message: "Sexuality is a sacred dimension of all our relationships; its fullest expression in sexual intercourse calls for a permanent covenant of mutual love." In other words, our focus needs to shift from the biological to the relational, from physical expression to interpersonal mutuality.

No matter what our vocational choice or our sexual orientation, we are called to live a life of chastity. Chastity is simply another word for the everyday face of love; it enables us to reverence the uniqueness and dignity of the other as friend, companion and partner.

Chastity: The Commitment to Partnership

If these reflections appear theoretical, perhaps some examples will illustrate the point more clearly. Let's suppose that an imaginary married couple, John and Mary, are celebrating their 25th anniversary. At a family gathering on the night before the celebration, John proudly tells his three children that he has always been faithful to his wife; he has never, as we say in our society, "stepped out" on her by having illicit sexual relations with anyone else. What John does not tell his children (even though it is probably fairly obvious), is that for 25 years he has treated Mary as though she were his servant girl. He expected to be waited on, catered to and obeyed; he reserved the right to make major decisions himself; he expected to have his sexual needs met without consideration of his wife; and if he died tomorrow, Mary would have little idea of their financial resources or how to manage them.

From a narrow, legalistic point of view, it might be possible to say that John has been faithful to his wife, but in the deepest sense he has not had a *chaste* relationship with her. He has not reverenced her as an equal partner or grown with her as a companion in a mutual covenant. There has not been, in the words of *Gaudium et Spes* (The Constitution on the Role of the Church in the Modern World), an "intimate partnership of life and love" (#48) in their marriage.

Let's examine a parallel example in celibate living. In this case, let's suppose that it is "Father Jim" who is celebrating his 25th anniversary of ordination. On the night before the festivities, Jim tells his confessor that he has always been faithful to celibacy; that he has never had sexual relations with anyone. What he does not share with his confessor is that he has also functioned as a "spiritual lone ranger" and that he is well on the way toward becoming a self-centered, cynical old bachelor. Jim treats the parish staff as though they were his hired help; he functions in a unilateral manner with little or no consultation; his parishioners experience him as a distant and lonely personality. Jim plays golf with a couple of fellow priests, travels on vacation and goes out to eat regularly, but he has no real friends. Nobody really knows his heart.

From a strictly canonical perspective, Jim may be faithful to his promise of celibacy, but, in the sense in which we are using the term, he is not living a *chaste* life. He has not developed the vulnerability that comes with friendship or the sense of partnership that flows from shared ministry. There is little evidence that he has invested in the demanding journey of self-disclosure and mutuality. His basic stance toward other people is that of control—either by distancing himself from them by his office, or by subtly dominating them in his style of leadership.

Dominative Power: The Sin Against Partnership

A few years ago, during the first three days of Holy Week, ABC Television aired the mini-series, *Thornbirds*, based on the novel of the same name by Colleen McCullough. Both the topic and the timing of the program prompted a strong negative reaction from several Catholic newspapers and not a few chancery offices. Many of the clergy warned their congregations, either from the pulpit or in the parish bulletin, not to watch the mini-series.

Ironically the advertisements that urged viewers to watch *Thornbirds* and the ecclesiastical warnings against it reflected a remarkably similar view of its theme: Do (as in the case of ABC) or do not (as in the case of some church officials) watch *Thornbirds* because it is the story of an illicit sexual relationship between Father Ralph and the young woman, Meggie. Those who were familiar with McCullough's novel were left wondering if the mini-series was based on the same book they had read. In the novel the sexual relationship between Father Ralph and Meggie is, at best, a sub-plot incidental to the primary drama. Ralph de Bricassart was indeed unfaithful to his promise of celibacy, but the deepest failure in his life was not a sexual one. Father Ralph's real sin was that he was willing to walk over anyone to get to the top, including the one woman who could have redeemed his life.

In the end, *Thornbirds* is not a story about an illicit sexual relationship; it is a story about claiming, controlling and climbing; it is a parable about the exploitive pursuit of power and the human brokenness that comes in its wake. It is significant that there were few, if any, voices among church leadership who objected to the mini-series on the basis that it portrayed the sinful pursuit of position and privilege. Perhaps this is because the institutional church has traditionally been more sensitive to the "hot sins" of passion than it has to the "cold sins" of calculation and injustice. In retrospect, church leaders might have done well to invite all their members to view the mini-series as a Lenten meditation; it is a striking reflection on the sinfulness of dominative power and our mutual need for redemption through authentic relationships.

Sexuality and Power

If partnership as a style of ministry is to continue to emerge in the church's life, we must overcome the two basic dualisms that have for so long prevented women and men from entering into a "discipleship of equals." The first dualism is the long-standing alienation between body and soul, flesh and spirit. It results in the lingering fear and suspicion we have toward sexuality. The second dualism is the "patriarchal assumption"—the perduring belief, whether implicit or explicit, that women are lower in dignity and importance than men. This dualism results in the feelings of oppression and alienation among women and the proclivity toward dominative power and spiritual impotence among men.

In a recent study, junior high school students were surveyed regarding their attitudes toward dating and sexuality. A surprising number of them, both girls and boys, thought that if a man spent money on a woman, taking her out to dinner and other forms of entertainment, he had a right to demand sexual favors in return. Other statistics reveal that these attitudes are not an isolated instance or an aberration in statistics. The incidents of sexual assault and date rape continue to rise; sexual molestation of children, wife battering and other forms of domestic violence are also widespread. The fact is that behind most sexual crimes the underlying passion is not sexual desire, but the drive to dominate, to control, to exploit and even to punish.

Sexuality and power—these two issues, as we have seen above, are deeply interrelated. They are issues that cannot be ignored if the church is to be *lumen gentium*— a light to the nations. The task of integrating sexuality and religious experience is one aspect of this challenge; the call to move beyond dominative power to shared responsibility is the other.

Intimacy and partnership—in some profound sense they are both the fertile soil and the testing ground for the gospel in our time. If the institutional church is willing to face these issues and to carry the implications into life, the renewal will deepen and flourish. If it avoids them or stands aside in fear, this moment of grace will have passed us by.

Select Bibliography

Bleier, Ruth. *Science and Gender*. New York: Pergamon Press, 1984.

Boff, Leonardo. *Jesus Christ Liberator: A Critical Christology for Our Time*. Maryknoll, NY: Orbis, 1978.

Boulding, Kenneth, as quoted in Elizabeth J. Hollins (ed.). *Peace Is Possible*. New York: Grossman, 1966.

Buhlmann, Walbert, O.F.M. Cap. *The Church of the Future*. Maryknoll, NY, and Melbourne, Australia: Orbis/Dove, 1986.

Burrows, William R. *New Ministries: The Global Context*. Maryknoll, NY: Orbis, 1980.

Durden-Smith, Jo, and deSimone, Diane. *Sex and the Brain*. New York: Warner Books, 1984.

Fausto-Sterling, Anne. *Myths of Gender: Biological Theories About Women and Men*. New York: Basic Books, Inc., 1985.

Fiorenza, Elisabeth Schussler. *In Memory of Her: A Feminist Theological Reconstruction of Christian Origins*. New York: Crossroad, 1983.

Flannery, Austin, O.P.,(Ed.) *Vatican Council II: The Conciliar and Post Conciliar Documents.* Northport, NY: Costello Publishing, 1975.

Gilligan, Carol. *In a Different Voice: Psychological Theory and Women's Development.* Cambridge: Harvard U. Press, 1982.

Heilbrun, Carolyn G. *Toward A Recognition of Androgyny.* New York: Harper Colophon Books, 1973.

Kennedy, Eugene C. "The Problem With No Name." *America.* Vol. 158, No. 16, April 23, 1988, 423-425.

Lee, Bernard J., and Cowan, Michael A. *Dangerous Memories: House Churches and Our American Story.* Kansas City, MO: Sheed and Ward, 1986.

Mateos, Juan. "The Message of Jesus." *Sojourners.* Vol.6, No. 8, pp. 8-16.

Matton, Mary Ann. *Jungian Psychology in Perspective.* New York: The Free Press, 1981.

McCullough, Colleen. *Thornbirds.* New York: Avon Books, 1979.

Meeks, Wayne. *The First Urban Christians: The Social World of the Apostle Paul.* New Haven and London: Yale U. Press, 1983.

Michener, James A. *Hawaii.* New York: Fawcett Crest, 1959.

National Conference of Catholic Bishops. "*Partners in the Mystery of Redemption: A Pastoral Response to Women's Concerns for Church and Society.*" First Draft. Washington, D.C.: USCC Publications, 1988.

Nelson, James B. *Between Two Gardens: Reflections on Sexuality and Religious Experience.* New York: Pilgrim Press, 1983.

Nelson, James B. "Reuniting Sexuality and Spirituality." *Christian Century,* Feb. 25, 1987, 187-190.

Nolan, Albert. *Jesus Before Christianity.* Maryknoll, NY: Orbis, 1978.

O'Brien, David J., and Shannon, Thomas A. (Eds.). *Renewing the Earth: Catholic Documents on Peace, Justice and Liberation.* Garden City, NY: Doubleday Image Books, 1977.

Osiek, Carolyn, R.S.C.J. *What Are They Saying About the Social Setting of the New Testament?* New York/Ramsey: Paulist, 1984.

Piaget, Jean. *The Moral Judgment of the Child.* New York: The Free Press, 1965.

Priests for Equality. "*Toward a Full and Equal Sharing: Pastoral Letter on Equality in the Church.*" West Hyattsville, MD, 1985.

Rahner, Karl. *Concern for the Church.* New York: Crossroad, 1981.

Ricoeur, Paul. "Wonder, Eroticism, and Enigma," in *Sexuality and Identity.* Hendrik M. Ruitenbeek (Ed.). New York: Dell, 1970.

Schillebeeckx, Edward. *The Church With a Human Face.* New York: Crossroad, 1985.

_____. *Ministry: Leadership in the Community of Jesus Christ.* New York: Crossroad, 1981.

Sehested, Nancy Hastings. "By What Authority Do I Preach?" *Sojourners,* Vol. 17, No. 2, February, 1988, p. 24.

Tetlow, Elisabeth M. *Women and Ministry in the New Testament.* New York: Paulist Press, 1980.

Trible, Phyllis. *God and the Rhetoric of Sexuality.* Philadelphia: Fortress Press, 1978.

Vawter, Bruce. *On Genesis.* Garden City, NY: Doubleday, 1977.